2024 - All rights reserved.

ontained within this book may not be reproduced,
transmitted without direct written permission from
the publisher.

cumstances will any blame or legal responsibility be
e publisher, or author, for any damages, reparation,
loss due to the information contained within this
irectly or indirectly.

Debt, Gun

(A Tale of how Debt Colle

Written by N

Copyright ©

The content
duplicated o
the author o

Under no ci
held against
or monetary
book, either

TABLE OF CONTENTS

Preface 1

Introduction 4

Chapter 1: You Need a Job 8

Chapter 2: The Talk Off 29

Chapter 3: From C.A. to G.A. 47

Chapter 4: Top Gun Collector (The Bonus Check) 70

Chapter 5: From Streets to Corporate Suites 103

Chapter 6: Party like a Boss (My own Shop) 132

Chapter 7: Stepping on the Product 159

Chapter 8: The Merchant 170

Chapter 9: Burn the client (Run off on The Plug) 184

Chapter 10: Some Extra Bread 204

Chapter 11: The Alphabet Boys 215

PREFACE

I dedicate this book to my Family, my Children, and my Real Homies. I love you all. This book is also dedicated to all the Top Gun Closers out there, who get up every morning and go to the office to get that money and that Bonus Check. I Salute you!

To all the professional debtors out there, who's constantly looking for ways to avoid paying their bills. Please don't attempt to use this book as ammo to add to your arsenal. Or, to help validate the excuses in your mind, for why you weren't paying your debts all along. If you're truly skeptical of the agency calling you, request a Validation of Debt letter and do some google's on the company. If you don't want to pay the damn bill, just admit it yourself and keep ducking and dodging us like you have been doing! Constantly changing your phone number and or screening calls. Just continue doing that for the next seven years until the debt falls off your credit. There, I helped you. Now, to all my collectors out there. Please don't call me, email me, DM me on social media, or rundown on me in public talking about: "Man, you was giving out way too much sauce in the book. Blah, blah, blah, you making it hard to get money out here." "Shut up! If the debt is valid, and your Talk Off and rebuttals are on point, you will get money regardless. After this is published, I will still be able to get in a cubicle and do numbers. So no excuses, just remember your A.B.C's (Always Be Closing.) Now that I got that out the way with.

I would like to say this book is in no way, shape, or form meant to expose, demean, or paint the debt collections industry or debt collectors in a negative light. If people paid their bills, there wouldn't be a need for debt collectors. Bare in mind, every industry within the corporate world, has an underbelly and loopholes that people exploit for financial gain. I'm simply pointing out some of the things that I've seen, heard and experienced.

Bill Collectors are unsung heroes in the economy. They're not annoying telemarketers. We are the ones that get people to pay their bills in which those funds are used to stimulate the economy and keep businesses open. Subsequently providing jobs for people, so on and so forth. No matter what I do in life or what field I end up in, I will always be a Top Gun Closer at heart. Some of the funnest times I ever had in my life was being in the office, drinking, closing deals, talking and cracking jokes with my coworkers in between calls.

If you ever worked with me before, you know how we do it.

Disclaimer

This story is loosely based on the truth and is for entertainment purposes. A huge percentage of its contents are fictional. Any resemblance to real life figures and characters is purely coincidental. Also, please note when reading the word "Nigga" which some may find offensive. Keep in mind, "Nigga is the universal name for young black men. It's like calling a white person dude" - Derek Grover (Author of "The Gang Bangers Dictionary")

Lastly, I would like to say Rest in Peace to Lanorva Thomas, she was a great collector with a heart of gold. I also would like to say Rest in Power to Byron Darden and Jeffrey McMillan. Two of the baddest Collectors in the game, and some of the coolest and funniest brothas I ever met. I learned a lot from you guys. Not just about collections, but about the game of life too.

INTRODUCTION

Debt, Guns and Dope.

This is a tale of how the debt collection industry can be just as cutthroat, dangerous, and vicious as the dope game. Depending on who you're doing business with or who you're getting your debt/ product from.

What's up world? My name is Lamont, but people in the office call me Monty, L Boogie, L, whatever. I'm 34 years old and I'm the owner of multiple collection agencies across North America. Some are brick and mortar, some agents work from home remotely. Now, don't get it fucked up. This ain't no fluffy kumbaya story about how a nigga from the hood became a young black business owner. Nah, this is a tale of how even in legal business, this shit is just like the streets.

Getting debt from a debt broker is similar to getting coke from the plug. You could spend cash up front or you can get it on consignment. In the collection industry, they usually do a 60/40 split, meaning the person giving you the debt keeps 60% and you keep 40% (of each payment collected). Just like in the dope game, you can step on the dope/step on the product. Meaning cut it with other substances to make more money, for those who've been under a rock for the last fifty years and haven't seen drug dealer movies. Well, in the collection industry, the debt can be stepped on just like Coke.

For example, say you want to buy some debt, somebody will sell you a portfolio for 5 to $10,000. What they will tell you is this debt portfolio has a $100,000 face value. What you don't understand is you won't make $100,000 back. Some of the accounts have been paid already. Some people have filed bankruptcy. Some people are RTPs—refusal to pay. Some people you would never get them on the phone. Also, what you don't know is these accounts are what we call beat up in the collections industry. Meaning, they have been called by hundreds of agents who have threatened them with court, warrants, or Lord knows what these hungry collectors have said to try to make them pay.

Anyways, you spend $10,000 on a portfolio with a $100,000 face value. Oh, did I mention that the same portfolio has been sold to five other game goofy agency owners just like you. Eager to make hundreds of thousands dollars off their measly 5 to 10 racks. You'll be lucky to even make your money back. You still have to pay your employees. You still have to pay for the office space every month, internet, the debt software, merchant fees (for processing payments), coffee, the list goes on and on.

Always remember, everyone in the collection industry is a smooth talker and master salesman.

We will get back to stepping on the product later, but just like in the dope game, not paying the plug back could have violent consequences. The same thing could happen in the collection industry with the debt broker. Failing to pay on time or not paying at all can have serious consequences. Just like in the streets, people aren't going to the police or filing lawsuits in court. Sometimes they come in with weapons and brute force to collect their money.

Stroll with me. Ima take you with me, on my treacherous journey to the top of the collection industry. Don't worry, I got your back.

CH:1 You need a Job!!

Mac Davenport

CHAPTER 1
YOU NEED A JOB

Debt /det/ noun

*Something, **typically money**, that is owed or due.*

- Webster's Dictionary

The year is 2007. At this time, I had just quit my job at Long John Silvers to pursue a rap career and try to be a rock star. I released a mixtape called "The Arrival" with the homie Snake P. I have been hustling on the streets full-time for over one year at this period selling weed, ecstasy pills, and CDs. Bootleg CDs were selling 3 CDs for $10, for the young bucks out there. That's how I made my money in those days. I had the city mapped out with certain spots that I would go to on certain days. I also had my clientele built up from the spots I would frequent.

One of my main money-making spots was the Walmart parking lot in College Grove. The whip I was pushing was a

1988 Cadillac Sedan DeVille, all black with shiny red leather interior sitting on 20-inch chrome wheels. Yeah. It also had the touchscreen, where the DVD player would pop out and then tuck away and hide back in the dash when you press the button.

Anyways, one day I was in the parking lot of Walmart doing my thing as usual. I had the trunk popped open with a box full of CDs and shooting my spiel at everybody that walked past. If they bought a CD, I would sniff them out and if I felt like they weren't Babylon or the police, I would let them know, "Hey, I got them thizzles and I got them trees." My aim was to get people to buy some of everything I got. This white boy wearing gray joggers, a white tee, silver chain and a hat turned to the back was walking to a black BMW parked across from me.

"Hey, bro, come check me out. I got the CDs, 3 for $10, and I got my new shit, The Arrival. I got the new Game, Lupe Fiasco, the new Jeezy." He walked towards me. He gave me a fist bump, looked down at the box of CDs in the trunk that was leaning against the spare tire. He said, "You said they were 3 for $10?" "Yep & if you support the movement and buy your boy's album, I'll toss in another one for free." He said, "How much do you want for your album?" I said, "I usually charge people like a hundred because the shit is just so slapping, but I'll throw it to you for $10." We chuckled. "You're a funny dude! Alright, I'm gonna rock with you, man." He reaches into his wallet and pulls out two 20's and hands them to me. "Keep the change." "Good looking. I appreciate that mane, what's your name?" "Aaron." "They call me Monty." Making eye contact. We bumped fist and he continued rummaging through the box of CDs to grab the ones that he wanted.

Debt, Guns, and Dope

He says, "Hey, you know where I can get some good bud?" Looking at him head to toe, as to read him for any signs of being an undercover. I said, "What you tryin to get?" "Just like an eighth." "I got you." I beelined my way to the driver's seat of the whip, and reached in my stash spot under the dashboard to grab the sandwich bag full of weed. Reaching under the seat, I pulled out a digital scale and dropped buds on it till it read 3.5g. Walking toward him, I reached my hand out to shake hands. In one motion, we shook and I released the weed filled receipt into his palm.

"Just slide me $30, bro," He handed me the money and smelled his palm. "Ooh, this smells like some fire." "It is. trust me! I got them thizzles too (Ecstasy Pills)." Unbeknownst to him, I was putting him through a test. I grabbed a half a blunt I had in my ashtray and I sparked it up. I took a few pulls of it and began coughing. "Here, this is what I just gave you" I set the blunt in between his white fingertips that sported dirty nails. Without hesitation, Aaron grabbed the blunt and said, "Hell yeah." he took a long slow drag. His face turned cherry red while holding in the smoke. "Whoo, Oh my God" he mumbled, coughing uncontrollably with smoke gushing out his mouth and nose. He patted his chest, urging me to take the blunt back. I did. "Take my number, I got that all day." We pulled off.

Debt, Guns, and Dope

Aaron was pretty cool. I used to serve him about once, sometimes twice a week. Trees, thizzles, and occasionally cocaine. I never had the coke on deck. However, I knew how to get it and where to get it for the low, so I would just grab some to make a flip off it from time to time. One day, he called saying he was trying to get like 10 pills and a quarter of weed (seven grams). I told him to meet me at the AMPM gas station on Home Avenue. It just so happens I wasn't driving my car that day. I was with the homie Doriano. We were out and about in traffic all day long that day.

After hanging up the phone, I asked the homie, "Ayy, can you shoot me to AMPM? I gotta make a tip." "I got you, shit.. just throw me like five on the tank." We pulled up to AMPM, to one of the pumps as though we were getting gas. I hopped out the passenger side of the car and slithered into the gas station to kill some time until Aaron pulled up. "Can I get five on pump number two, and a box of regular swishers? Thank you." The gas attendant, "Can I see some ID?" She glanced at my ID and handed it right back. I cashed her out. "Have a great day." Pumping the gas and scanning every car that pulled into the parking lot, he finally pulled up.

"There he go," I told the homie, letting go of the gas nozzle trigger. Aaron nodded his head, "What's up Monty" with a white guy in the passenger seat that I'd never seen before. He appeared to be in his mid-20s. I walked to Aarons side of the truck and I dropped a bag of weed and the pills on his lap. We shake hands, and he hands me the money folded up in his palm. Cuffing the money, I drop it in my pocket in a natural motion. "All right bro, hit me later," I said, walking off briskly. They pulled out of the parking lot with us trailing behind them.

Once in the car, I fastened my seatbelt, pulled out my phone and toggled between playing games and text messaging. The homie drove real quiet, real solemn and was looking extremely serious. He didn't say anything for the whole ride. He just glanced at me out of the corner of his eyes from time to time. A few minutes away from my house, he finally broke the silence. "Hey, where you meet him at?" "Shit, at the Walmart." "Man…that nigga the police, He's an undercover bro" My heart sank to my stomach. The homie had a look on his face, like he knew something bad was going to happen to me. We pulled up in front of my house, we slapped hands and I hopped out of the car. "Yo man, you trying to come in and get yo ass whooped on some of this Madden?" The homie, "Nah, I'm good G, be careful with that muthafucka though- don't serve him nothing else!" The homie pulled off.

I couldn't stop thinking about what he said. I was paranoid about my house getting raided, and I couldn't believe that I've been serving an undercover agent for months. "Im Stupid!" "Fuck im going to prison." "I should have been taking my ass to the Masjid with grandpops" My mind was racing with thoughts. After pondering on it, I came up with the idea to rob him next time he called. A few weeks later, on a Friday afternoon, I did just that.

Chapter 1: You Need a Job

Two, almost three weeks have passed by with me not hearing from Aaron. I found it strange because normally I served him at least once, maybe twice a week. Anyways, I was listening to Mac Dre "Genie of the Lamp" and edging up my mustache when my Sidekick rang. It was him! He said he was trying to get 2,000 pills. I already had my plan mapped out that I was going to rob him next time I talked to him. I told him to meet me at the Walmart. I had my uncle Freddy Red take me to meet him. My plan was to get him to the John Adams Projects.

John Adams, is a large apartment complex with over 500 units. Broken down into multiple buildings and sections throughout acres of land. It has multiple entrances and exits that lead to different side streets and buildings. You can walk through the various trails, alleys, and breezeways to end up on a completely different side of the apartments and or different building.

We met up with Aaron at the Walmart. I had my uncle Freddy Red drive me over there. My plan was to pick him up, and get him inside the projects. Once there, get him to hand me the money and I'm to get out of the car. Once I'm out of the car, call him and tell him to come choose what pills he wants. Being that my imaginary plug has a variety of flavors (different colors, mdma levels, double stack or triple stack pills). When he got out of the car, I had already gained Aarons trust. He would hand me the money before getting his pills sometimes, and I would come back with them. Anyways, once he got his snake ass out of the car, my uncle is supposed to pull off and drive around to the backside of the projects to pick me up on Grape St. By that time, my phone would be cut off and I would be cutting through the alley so Freddy Red can scoop me up. I figured we would just leave him and go on about our day.

Aaron was now in the back seat, unaware of what's about to happen to him. We picked him up from Walmart just as planned. It was a quiet ride. All his questions and concerns were met with one word answers. I know I didn't have that volume of pills. I didn't even know anybody that sold pills in John Adams. Finally, we arrived. We cruised in the parking lot and halted in front of the staircase, of the huge brown complex that read "Building C units: 200- 300" Without turning around, from the passenger seat. I said "Aight, we're here bro" looking around nervously, he replied "How much does he want for them?" "It's gone be $2,000 or like $1 a pill. Shit, he's actually showing you some love on the ticket (price)" He nodded his head in agreement. I had closed the deal! He reached in the front seat handing me the stack of wrinkled one hundred dollar bills. Which I later found out was marked money. I hopped out of the car and began my trek up the four flights of stairs. It was a long four flight of stairs, like going up the stairway to heaven. I finally got to the very top. Out of breath I start making my way towards the alley. I called Aaron. In an excited tone I said "Hey man, my plug has like four or five different kinds up here! You need to come see these homie, Come up here and pick out flavors you want."

Aaron gets out of the car, just as planned. As he's walking up the flight of stairs. Freddy Red skirts off (Tires screeching) and drives to the back of the complex to Grape ST. By this time my phone was off and I was already half way through the alley, to meet him. A helicopter was circling in the sky the whole time I was making my move. I didn't think anything of it though. This is Southeast San Diego. Between the gangs and all the shit that goes on, I just figured they were out doing their job. I never imagined it was there for little old me. Although, the whole time it did seem as though it was

Debt, Guns, and Dope

trailing me. I just brushed it off as paranoia. I shook my uncle's hand and slid him a couple of hundred dollars out of the stack. "Wooooo, hey man, let's go get some weed, we need to hit Par Liquor, let's get a bottle!" I said feeling like I just pulled off a million dollar heist. My uncle smiled, and merged on the freeway that read 15 North. I continued, "Shit, we can go grab something to eat, food on me today!.."

After about two miles of driving, we get ambushed by San Diego Police cars and undercover cops in unmarked cars. It was Black cops and White cops in plain clothes with badges and guns all working together with the uniformed police and the feds. "FREEZE, FREEZE, get out the FUCKING car." "Put your hands where I can see them." They aggressively yelled. With a Glock pointing at my face. They snatched us out of the car and handcuffed us one by one. The first thing the babylon (police) did after reading me my rights, was reach in my front pocket and pull out the marked one hundred dollar bills. They had given Aaron the money to purchase the pills from me. It turns out he was an undercover cop for the San Diego Police Department. They were in the middle of a sting, attempting to clean up the streets. One of my homeboys got caught up in the same sting with a few kilos of coke last year. It was actually the homie that told me, Aaron looked like the police. Ain't that some shit!? I wasn't the only one who got jammed up that year though. The feds were busy in Daygo and across the U.S. This just so happened to be the year they bagged Bernie Madoff. Bernard Lawrence Madoff was an American financial criminal and financier who was the admitted mastermind of the largest known Ponzi scheme in history, worth an estimated $65 billion. Also, in May of 2008 over 100 students were arrested at San Diego State University in a drug raid. Students and some non-students, were arrested and handed drug charges, after undercover federal agents blended in on campus. They ended up seizing over 350 ecstasy pills, four pounds of cocaine, and about 50 pounds of weed. The drug sweep landed members of three fraternities in jail and led to the suspension of six frats, investigators revealed. Campus police had started an investigation, a year prior, after a student fatally overdosed in May of 2007. NBC, CNN, The New York Times, and The L.A. Times covered the story.

IN CUSTODY

SUPERIOR COURT OF CALIFORNIA, COUNTY OF SAN DIEGO
CENTRAL DIVISION

THE PEOPLE OF THE STATE OF CALIFORNIA,
                                              Plaintiff,
              v.
LAMONT ALI MADYUN,
   dob 01/10/86, Booking No. 08114775.A;
FRED
   dob 01   Booking No. 08114776.A,
   aka FRED
                                              Defendants

CT No. CD212106
DA No. ACF490

COMPLAINT-FELONY

INFORMATION

Date: 5-28-08

PC296 DNA TEST STATUS SUMMARY

Defendant	DNA Testing Requirements
MADYUN, LAMONT ALI	DNA sample required upon conviction
, FRED	DNA sample required upon conviction

CHARGE SUMMARY

Count	Charge	Issue Type	Sentence Range	Special Allegations	Allegation Effect
1	HS11379(a) MADYUN, LAMONT ALI	Felony	2-3-4		
2	HS11379(a) MADYUN, LAMONT ALI , FRED	Felony	2-3-4		
3	PC487(a) MADYUN, LAMONT ALI , FRED	Felony	16-2-3		

PC1054.3   INFORMAL REQUEST FOR DISCOVERY

Page 1 of 3, Court Case No. CD212106

The undersigned, certifying upon information and belief, complains that in the County of San Diego, State of California, the Defendant(s) did commit the following crime(s):

CHARGES

COUNT 1 - SELL/FURNISH CONTROLLED SUBSTANCES

On or about February 12, 2008, LAMONT ALI MADYUN did unlawfully sell, furnish, administer and give away and offer to sell, furnish, administer and give away controlled substances, to wit: 3-4 methylenedioxymethamphetamine ("MDMA"; "Ecstasy"), an analog of methamphetamine, within the meaning of Health and Safety Code Section 11401, in violation of HEALTH AND SAFETY CODE SECTION 11379(a).

COUNT 2 - SELL/FURNISH CONTROLLED SUBSTANCES

On or about February 28, 2008, LAMONT ALI MADYUN and FRED███████████████ did unlawfully sell, furnish, administer and give away and offer to sell, furnish, administer and give away controlled substances, to wit: 3-4 methylenedioxymethamphetamine ("MDMA"; "Ecstasy"), an analog of methamphetamine, within the meaning of Health and Safety Code Section 11401, in violation of HEALTH AND SAFETY CODE SECTION 11379(a).

COUNT 3 - GRAND THEFT OF PERSONAL PROPERTY

On or about February 28, 2008, LAMONT ALI MADYUN and FRED███████████████ did unlawfully take and steal money and personal property of CS-0196, of a value in excess of Four Hundred Dollars ($400), in violation of PENAL CODE SECTION 487(a).

NOTICE: Any defendant named on this complaint who is on criminal probation in San Diego County is, by receiving this complaint, on notice that the evidence presented to the court at the preliminary hearing on this complaint is presented for a dual purpose: the People are seeking a holding order on the charges pursuant to Penal Code Section 872 and simultaneously, the People are seeking a revocation of the defendant's probation, on any and all such probation grants, utilizing the same evidence, at the preliminary hearing. Defenses to either or both procedures should be considered and presented as appropriate at the preliminary hearing.

Pursuant to PENAL CODE SECTION 1054.5(b), the People are hereby informally requesting that defendant's counsel provide discovery to the People as required by PENAL CODE SECTION 1054.3.

The People reserve the right to amend the accusatory pleading to further allege any and all facts in aggravation in light of Cunningham v. California (2007).

Sheriff's records indicate that as of the booking date one or more defendants have not yet provided a DNA sample to the DOJ database. Pursuant to Penal Code Section 296(e), the court shall order collection of DNA from the defendant(s) if advised by the prosecuting attorney that a sample is required but has not been provided by the defendant. Pursuant to Penal Code sections 296/296.1, if not already required from a past conviction, any defendants who have not done so will be required to provide a sample upon conviction of this felony offense.

Page 2 of 3, Court Case No. CD212106

Debt, Guns, and Dope

Lexington National Insurance Corporation
200 East Lexington Street • Suite 501
Baltimore, MD 21202
(410) 625-0800

SWAFFORD'S BAIL BONDS
5073 LOGAN AVE
SAN DIEGO, CA 92113
(619) 262-0409 . (619) 269-5560
LIC BA 1842531

BAIL BOND No. 2008-BB-007758
(POWER OF ATTORNEY WITH THIS NUMBER MUST BE ATTACHED.)

IN THE **Superior** COURT OF THE **Central Division** JUDICIAL DISTRICT
COUNTY OF **San Diego**, STATE OF CALIFORNIA
THE PEOPLE OF THE STATE OF CALIFORNIA

Case No. **CD212106**
Plaintiff,
Div. No. **#29**

VS

Lamont Madyun
Defendant

Defendant **Lamont Madyun** (Booking No.) **8114775**
having been admitted to bail in the sum of **Ten thousand dollars**
Dollars ($ **10,000.00**) and ordered to appear in the above-entitled court
on **3-12-At 8:15 a.m.** 20 **08**, on **11379 HS x 2, 487 (A) PC** charge/s:

Now the LEXINGTON NATIONAL INSURANCE CORPORATION, a Maryland Corporation, hereby undertakes that the above-named defendant will appear in the above-named court on the date above set forth to answer any charge in any accusatory pleading based upon the acts supporting the complaint filed against him/her and all duly authorized amendments thereof, in whatever court it may be prosecuted, and will at all times hold him/herself amenable to the orders and process of the court, and, if convicted, will appear for pronouncement of judgement or grant of probation; or, if he/she fails to perform either of these conditions, that the LEXINGTON NATIONAL INSURANCE CORPORATION, a Maryland Corporation, will pay to the people of the State of California, the sum of
Ten thousand dollars Dollars ($ **10,000.00**).
If the forfeiture of this bond be ordered by the Court, judgement may be summarily made and entered forthwith against the said LEXINGTON NATIONAL INSURANCE CORPORATION, a Maryland Corporation, for the amount of its undertaking herein, as provided by Sections 1305 and 1306 of the California Penal Code.

THIS BOND IS VOID IF WRITTEN FOR AN AMOUNT GREATER THAN THE POWER OF ATTORNEY ATTACHED HERETO. IF MORE THAN ONE SUCH POWER IS ATTACHED, OR IF WRITTEN AFTER THE EXPIRATION DATE SPECIFIED ON THE ATTACHED POWER OF ATTORNEY.

LEXINGTON NATIONAL INSURANCE CORPORATION

By *Charles Swafford*

I certify under penalty of perjury that I am a licensed bail Agent of the LEXINGTON NATIONAL INSURANCE CORPORATION and that I am executing this bond on **3-4-08** (date)
at **5073 Logan Ave, San Diego, CA, 92113** (location)
Charles Swafford (signature of licensed agent)

The Premium Charged for this Bond is
$ **1,000.00**

Approved this **4th** day of **March**, 20 **08**
R. Labrada
Title

Mad Davenport

When I bailed out of jail, my girlfriend at the time was furious with me. I was living under her roof, but I wasn't contributing to the rent. I didn't have any bread to put on the groceries. Plus, I was driving her car and smoking up all her weed. Just leeching off her at the moment, and it became obvious. She yelled "I CAN NOT TAKE THIS SHIT NO MORE LAMONT! you need to get a FUCKING JOB!" She was fed up with me. She threw the San Diego Union-Tribune at me. The classifieds section to be exact. While skimming through it, I saw a job for debt collections. I didn't know what the hell debt collection was. I circled it anyway. It was starting off at $17 an hour. I figured, "Hey, I'll stand at a window, people will walk in to make payments, and I'll just give them a receipt." It sounded easy enough. I never knew what I was getting myself into. I applied for the job at QRS Services, and actually landed it with my mouth piece and quick wits. I interviewed with two managers before finally meeting and interviewing with the owner of the company. He took a liking to me. A retired football player from the NFL, He said, "You know what, kid? I'm going to give you a shot." And there I began my collection journey.

CH 2: THE TALK OFF

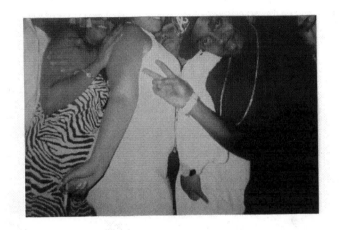

Mad Davenport

GC Services

8400 Miramar Road, Ste 250
San Diego, California 92126

May 23, 2008

To Whom It May Concern:

The reason for my letter is to acknowledge the established creditability and character for Lamont Madyun. He is an individual that I can count on both personally and professional. I have trust in his judgment and his decision making.

I work in an industry that forces me to be very selective in people I can rely on which has helped me create a knack for identifying individual qualities. Lamont is the type that people are drawn to not only because he is loyal but because he is dedicated to whatever task he encounters. Whether it's a personal or professional goal, I can attest to his motivation and drive to accomplish it and ensure it is done to the highest standard. Lamont is a very creative person and is not afraid to take risks that will benefit his goals. He is organized, takes criticism well, and exudes focus and attention to detail.

All in all Lamont comes highly recommended and has easily fit into my organization. He is considered a valuable asset and I am glad to have him as part of my team.

Regards,

Richard D. Watts
Manager

CHAPTER 2
THE TALK OFF

The world is a Talk Off. It's like the Da Vinci Code of Words. Saying the right combination, at the right time to unlock material results.

-Lamont Davenport

My grandma always told me, you got a line for everybody. She wasn't lying. I was always quick-witted, able to respond to any joke, question, insult, or whatever at lightning speed. I never knew in the future that these abilities would take me to places I never imagined. I just always like to talk shit. Plus, you got to have jokes and be quick when you grew up like me. I was short and dark with crooked teeth. I was low-hanging fruit for anybody that wanted to roast. But I always had rebuttals. Today is Sunday, and tomorrow I start my new job at QRS Services. I was told by the boss that they dress business casual Monday through Thursday, and Friday is casual day. No shorts. They emphasised that. The job was across the street from Miramar Air Base, where they filmed the movie Top Gun in the '80s with Tom Cruise. I didn't have any dress clothes or casual clothes to wear, so I called the best person I knew who had that apparel, my grandfather. My grandfather was a devout Muslim, and he wore suits most of the time. I called to see if he could let me borrow a tie, a few dress shirts, and a few pairs of slacks. I called him.

"Assalam-o-Alaykum." "Hey, pops!" "Hey, Monty. What's going on, son?" "Nothing much. Guess what, pops? I got a job!" "Oh, congratulations, man. Doing what?" "Debt collections." "Oh, I got to tell your grandma. Shahidah, Monty got a job!" "Oh, that's wonderful!" Grandmoms cheered in the background. "Hey, pops. The reason I called is, Can I borrow a few dress shirts and slacks and things like that?" "Yeah, no problem. I got a few things I can give you. Come on by." "I appreciate it. All right, pops. See you in a second." "All right. Assalam-o-Alaykum." "Wa-Alaykum-Assalam."

On the way to my grandparents' house, I stopped by Green Cat liquor to get a few dollar shots. Then I hit the taco shop across the street to grab a Carne Asada Burrito. When I got to my grandparents' house, grandpops was outside watering the grass. I pulled in the driveway. "Hey, son!" He gave me a hug and held the back of my head, to crown the hook in my head. He always smelled like frankincense and mur oils or expensive cologne. "Hey, pops, where grandma at?" "She in there." I walked in the house and gave my grandma a tight hug and a kiss on the cheek.

"How are you doing, baby?" "Im doing good. Happy I finally landed a job" "Yes, Papa told me. I'm proud of you Monty! and it's so good to see you!" Grandmoms was always happy to see me. "Aww, Thanks. You too, Grams! It smells good in here." I loved going to my grandparents' house. My grandparents raised me. I grew up there. I was in between their home as well as my mom's. My grandpa walked in. "Come on, let me see what I got for you." I followed him down the flight of three stairs to their bedroom. My grandma trailed behind us. "All right, pops, don't be giving me none of that leftover gear from the '70s that you can't get rid of" Grandmoms giggled. "Hey, listen, listen. Beggars can't be choosers." He looked through his drawer for a sec, then turned around and entered the walk in closet shared by him and grandmoms. He swiped from left to right. Observing his shirts, jeans, blazers, button downs and slacks. The look on his face said he was trying to evaluate what to part ways with.

"All right Uhm.. you can have this." He handed me a plain white button down shirt, a blue and white polo, a pair of khakis, and black slacks. "Grab those boots right there, and those brown loafers." After a couple of minutes of going through grandpops wardrobe, I tracked out from my grandparents' house.

While rolling in reverse, grandmoms said, "Please be safe out there. Somebody just got killed at Euclid trolley station the other day" "I will, grandma.. Alright bye, see you guys later." They waved bye in a duet as I pulled off. I got home anxious to start my new job. I woke up the next morning, had a cup of coffee, and stopped by Jack in the Box on the way to work for breakfast. When I got to work, I found out that debt collections was nothing like I thought. I was actually going to be calling people over the phone to collect the delinquent debt. Meaning, if someone didn't pay their credit card bill, I would be the one calling them to collect that payment. It was my duty to negotiate and set up a payment arrangement that's feasible for their budget. I also was collecting on small instalment loans. If someone took out a $5,000 loan, and did not adhere to their monthly payments, I would call them and set up a payment plan. To officially be a part of the company I had to complete a 3-week training class. The first two weeks had absolutely nothing to do with talking itself. I was learning the F.D.C.P.A. The F.D.C.P.A is the Fair Debt Collections Practices Act. It's the main body of laws and regulations that governs Debt Collectors and collection agencies to ensure they're not doing unfair, deceptive, abusive acts or practices to collect the debt from you.

Making sure they're not threatening you or in so many words just saying anything wild or crazy to get you to pay the debt. In collections, you have to be F.D.C.P.A certified to work with these agencies. The F.D.C.P.A is the reason why no one can call you before 08:00 AM in the morning or after 09:00 PM in the evening. Per the F.D.C.P.A, people are not allowed to leave multiple messages in one day or just harass you and call you. They're the reason that certain laws are in place when it comes to dealing with you as a consumer and/or debtor.

Aside from learning the FDCPA, I also had to learn how to navigate their collection software. Meaning the software that houses the debt. Or, where you see the debtor's name on the computer screen. How to find the screen that shows where they were employed, the interest rate on the loan, their social security number, and all of the pertinent information that is needed to collect the debt. Also, where to notate the account. Every encounter that you have with the debtor or consumer on the phone, must be notated. This way you can keep a profile on a person and know exactly who you're dealing with, and what has been discussed in previous conversations. I spent a week doing F.D.C.P.A training, and the second week learning how to navigate their collection software. We also learned a little bit about the history of the company.

Any who, my last week of training, I finally learned what it's all about, the talk-off. A talk-off is a term that's used in collections or sales. Call Centers and telemarketers marketing companies use the term also, but it refers to the delivery of a script or a pitch. For instance, we all have gotten telemarketing calls or had a cheesy salesman try to sell us something over the phone. Well, they're using a script or a talk off. They will call you and say, "Hello!" very energetic.

"My name is Tom! I'm with ABC Cruise Services. How would you like a free cruise for two to the Caribbean?" Or the bill collector who calls you very low and stern with his tone and says, "My name is Doug. I represent ABC Services. The nature of this call is to inform you there's a pending civil suit that may be filed against you for an unpaid short-term loan." Although these are two totally different types of calls, industries, and approaches, they all have one thing in common. They use a Talk-Off.

Chapter 2: The Talk Off

A script where every word and tone of voice is accounted for is like a science, saying the right thing at the right time in the right tone of voice. Also, knowing when to pause, or as they say, the psychological pause, leaving some dead air for the words to swirl around the consumer or a debtor's head and let them ponder on what you just said. The trick is talking again at the right moment, because if done wrong, the pause is too long. They will think you forgot what you're talking about, and you might come across as dumb or slow. When someone calls you or approaches you, they know the exact tone to use, when to talk louder or sigh and talk lower, depending on the topic. They also know the exact words to use and are equipped with rebuttals or an answer for any questions, pushbacks, concerns, or whatever. The best closers are the ones with great tone, good diction, quick wits, delivery, and rebuttals. The sharper the rebuttals, the stronger the closer. After reading the script verbatim, learning how to talk off, and shadowing the collectors that've been there for a while, Shadowing means sitting right next to them and watching their daily workflow and listening and learning how they handle calls.

While shadowing the Closers, I realized I have been talking off my whole time hustling on the streets and not realizing it. When selling CDs, drugs, or trying to get someone to buy something you have, you're using a script or a pitch. The world is a Talk Off. It's like the Da Vinci Code of Words, saying the right combination at the right time to unlock results on the physical plane. After my three-week training was completed, I felt like I graduated college or something. We had to pass an exam containing everything we learned over the past three weeks. I finally was on the floor. We were finally official, no longer in the conference room, reading, learning things, and taking practice tests. We were finally out there with the top dogs, the closers. It is intimidating when you hear some of these people's delivery on the phone, and how good they are at what they do. I shadowed one of the best collectors in the office. It was a woman named Butter. She was light skinned, but they called her Butter because her talk off was as smooth as butter. Also, once she got to talking, she was on a roll. We walked towards her cubicle where she had pictures of her husband and kids hanging up. On her desk was a bag of Hot Cheetos and a box of Newports. She also had all the scripts hung up along with sticky notes that had different rebuttals.

I pulled up a computer chair next to her. "Have a seat." She said. As I sat down, I could hear other people in the cubicle next over. "No, no, no, ma'am. Okay. Well, listen, you shouldn't have taken the loan out if you couldn't afford to pay it back." Butter said, "Don't worry about him. He is doing all that and making all that noise, but he ain't getting no money. Have you ever done collections before?" "No, this is my first time." "Okay, so you have a lot to learn." She clicked on the keyboard a few times and logged into the system. Her phone rang. "Oh, wait, hold on. I got a call." "QRS Services. How may I help." She said. I couldn't make out what the man was saying. She pulled up his account. "Okay. Is this Mr. Andres?" "Yes, this is him." "All right. It looks like you have an outstanding balance of $576.19. Are you prepared to pay that right now?" "No, I don't have a job."

She quickly rebuttaled. "Okay. Are you still receiving unemployment benefits?" "No ma'am" She leaned forward. "Well, sir, how are you taking care of yourself? Give me one second." She put him on hold. She let me know this man was using a stalling tactic, and he was lying about receiving unemployment benefits.

She pulled up his skip report in the system Accurint. It showed that Mr. Andres actually had a job. A skip report shows your background, assets, employment data, ect. She unmuted the phone."Okay, sir, so you're not working at Premier Landscaping Services? It shows here that you're a full-time employee." "Okay, I work there sometimes." "You know what, sir?" She cut him off. "You're starting off this conversation on the wrong foot. You could have just been honest with me. How much can you pay today?" I don't have anything today."

"I know you have something?" I noticed how she was like a shark in the water, smelling blood. She smelt money within him. I would have given up on the call." I have no money. I promise" plead Mr.Andres. "Okay, what about your spouse? You don't have your mom?, anyone that can assist you? Is your wife not working as well?" His wife took the phone. "Ma'am, we don't have much money to spare. Can you guys work with us? We can do $300 today, will you take it?" "Give me one second." She put them on hold again to let them sizzle. I'm looking at her like, Wow, this lady's a Wizard.

After letting them sizzle for a few moments, she took them off of hold. "All right, I'm going to accept that today. We'll do a settlement offer. If you can do $350 right now, we'll write the rest off as an acceptable loss." "Oh, thank you so much, ma'am." The lady said with gratitude.

"Okay, go ahead and get your credit card or debit card." She grabbed her debit card and began reading Butter the numbers.

After getting the credit card number and processing the payment, She said "All right, ma'am, your payment has been processed. I'm going to send a receipt to you via email. I'm also going to send you a Settled in Full letter. It's not considered paid in full, because you paid a reduced amount. However, it will reflect settled in full on your credit report. We do report to all three credit bureaus." "All right. Thank you so much!" The lady repeated.

"All right, ma'am. Well, you have a great day." She hung up the phone, and looked over at me. "And that's how you do it."

Until this day, she's still one of the most incredible Closers, I've ever been around.

Chapter 2: The Talk Off

Butter stood up and uttered "I need a cigarette." patting the top of her head. At that moment, I noticed the Top Gun Closers, which she was, meant that she hit her budget and collected more money than everyone in the office. They were able to take more breaks than everybody else. Also, they walked around the office and did what they wanted to. Came in late and didn't get chastised. While the person who didn't hit their goal or had low numbers was always in the hot seat, always under the gun of being fired. Debt Collections is a production-based business. I learned early on that no matter how much they like you, no matter how cool you are, no matter how punctual you are, if you're not hitting your numbers, you can potentially get fired. It's all about the money in Debt Collections. When you hit your budget, you walk around the office and you're getting praised, you got a bonus check, everybody loves you. It's all smiles, and it's all good from the manager because they get a percentage of you hitting your budget, so they're incentivized to make sure that you collect a lot of money.

But the next month, if you don't hit your budget, it's cold stares, it's not many smiles, and it's a whole lot of "What's going on with you?" "What's going on with your numbers?" You always feel under pressure when your numbers aren't up. QRS Services was a very compliant collection agency. They didn't violate the F.D.C.P.A, and I really learned the rules and regulations of how collections work. After shadowing butter for a few days, I finally got my own cubicle. I liked QRS Services. It was a professional work environment and everybody was really cool, especially my manager. But I wasn't taking it seriously. I was only 21 years old at the time. I would go out to the club, party all night. Drinking, popping E pills, smoking, trying to pursue a one-night stand. Leave Club Mystery in Tijuana, Mexico at five o'clock in the morning, stand in line at the border for an hour eating a bacon wrapped hotdog and then drive 45 minutes straight to work. When I got there I slept in the parking lot for an hour, and then woke up to go to work. Basically, working from 8am - 5pm, off of three hours of sleep. Oh yeah, I also would sleep in the break room on my 15-minute breaks and doze off at my desk. To have enough juice to get through the rest of the shift, I used my one hour lunch break to eat a little something (trying to soak up alcohol) before going to sleep in my Cadillac.

I would come in late, and call out all the time. I didn't give a shit, I was a wild boy! All I cared about was having enough money for studio time, weed, and partying with the homies. Besides, I didn't have any major bills or responsibilities. Looking back, I really wasn't taking that job seriously, like I should have. One Wednesday, I was at work dozing off as the phone was ringing. I kept getting phone calls over and over and over on my cell. I finally answered. It was the Homie Sean Cheese. I whispered "Hello." He excitedly shouted in my ear. "Ayy, come outside, nigga!" "What!? You outside? Alright here I come." I put my phone in the meeting disposition and slithered out of the office. Walking down the flight of stairs, I see the homie, Sean Cheese, Johnny Castro, and Trav Action (Rest in Power), leaned up against the Silver BMW 325i. They were passing a blunt in rotation while choking and laughing. They looked happy and relaxed as a muthafucka. Like they just got off a cruise from the Bahamas, and had a few million on em. Energy just on ten. They were flossing new Coogi and Ed Hardy. Had on gold chains and watches, standing there with hella swag. Nipsey Hussle's "Hussle In The House", was blaring out of the car speakers. I didn't know who Nip (Rest in Power) was at that time. "Ayy, ya'll niggas turn that shit down, man, and tap that blunt out! You trying to get me fired or somethin?" Coughing, the homie Sean said "Man, fuck that job. How much they paying you up there?" I scoffed "Nigga, don't worry about that." The homie was a master salesman. He made his money doing face-to-face sales. The type of salesman that would run up on you in a parking lot.

He had a master salesman Talk Off. Anyways, he said "Whatever man, fuck all that. We got a business opportunity for you." They had got a storage unit, and they copped thousands of dollars worth of merchandise. They were moving to Los Angeles, with plans to start a business selling merch throughout the city. He continued "Man, Travs Cousin lives out there on King and Bud Long. He said we can crash at his gates" Johnny spoke his peace. "Everything gone be silky smooth cutty, we gone eat sellin this merch. I'm telling you! And you gone be your own boss!" Sean piggy backed off his point "We could take this shit all around the world homie! We gone start off in L.A., then hit Vegas, then the Bay. Shit, after that we'll probably hit the East Coast. You know I got family in New York " Johnny picked back up "We gone make millions Monty, come work wit us. You know you want to. Man, fuck that job!" Smoke rushed out of his mouth as he smiled. Sean put the icing on the cake "Ohh.. I know what this nigga need to see. He think we playin. Hold up.

Here" Reaching in his pocket he pulls a out a Cheddar Knot (wad of cash) and hands me like 160 bucks. "Go head and put that in ya pocket. That's chump change homie. I probably was gone give that to the homeless, or spend it on some ice cream or something." They had me thinking about it. "Man, quit wasting time." Trav chimed in calmly, "Bro, You could be making $300 a day fucking with us." Sean interrupted "Oh, I get it! Now you wanna be Mr. Company man? With them tight-ass slacks on." They busted out laughing in unison. I glanced down at the slacks that grandpops gave me. He picked up where he left off "Yeah, I know that's your grandpa's shirt too, nigga. Out here Lookin like a civil rights leader." He giggled. I smirked and looked off into the sunset. I wanted to return fire, but he was too fresh and I didn't have anything. I had to retreat. "I'll think about it homie" I said. The homie Trav closed things out like the voice of reason. "Listen, you don't have nothing to worry about. We gone make sure you straight bro. We already got a place to stay, we gonna make sure you eat and got money in your pockets. My other relly (relative) lives in Long Beach, we gone stay at her gates too sometimes. We wouldn't be here if we didn't need you, Monty." Trav was speaking calmly and rationally. He said "The storage unit is already full of merch. We goin back up there this weekend too. You can slide wit us to see how it goes" I didn't even realise they were talking me off right there in my job parking lot. It did sound enticing. I'm at work, tired, and these niggas is on their own time, riding around, smoking chronic, buying new clothes, and doing what they want to. "All right, man, I got to get back up here." We slapped hands. "Yeah, nigga, get back up there before you get fired" They all laughed. "Whatever, cantaloupe head ass nigga! I'll hit ya'll up later." I ran back upstairs before my manager noticed I was on an unauthorised break. I didn't quit that day, but a couple of days later, I did put in my two-week notice, and that was the end of me working at QRS Services.

CH: 3 FROM C.A. TO G.A.

MAd DAvenport

CHAPTER 3
FROM C.A. TO G.A.

"Be safe out there Blood. Let niggaz know, If anything happens to you. The homies is comin and we layin Shit Down! One love."

-One of the Homies

"Ay, spot me." I said, to the homie Derrick, laying down on the dusty weight bench that sat under a palm tree. We were in his grandma's backyard lifting weights and taking shots of Hennessy in between reps.

Me and Derrick grew up together. His grandmoms lived a few houses up the block from mines in a neighborhood called Emerald Hills. A Blood neighborhood that flies gray flags. "Throw another 45 plate on there." He sarcastically said, knowing damn well I couldn't hit two 45 plates (225 pounds including the bar). I was only weighing a buck 40, plus I was in terrible shape: between the fast food diet, late nights and early mornings, staying up all night clubbing, going to work early in the morning, constant use of weed, liquor, and thizzles. It's a miracle my arms didn't snap with one 45 plate on each side.

I gripped the bar and began my reps. Looking down at me and tapping the bar with his fingertips to help me see the rep through, Derrick blurted out, "Man, you really quit your job to move to LA and sell kid toys with them niggas?" "Yep." I replied, dropping the bar on the steel J-shaped hooks. I sat up and caught my breath, panting. I replied, "I already put in my two week notice. This Friday's my last day." He shook his head "Nigga, yo ass is stupid. You never leave your Fa Sho money. That shit ain't guaranteed dough. You was getting the check every two weeks, benefits, PTO, all that. You should have kept that job."

Although we were the same age, the homie was more mature and more responsible than me. He already had a son, his own apartment, and he was in a committed relationship with his high school sweetheart, soon to be married. He had his head on straight.

Cutting him off, I said, "Well it's too late nigga. Besides, I'm about to be my own boss." In the back of my mind, I knew he was right, but I had already made my decision and I was committed to it. I found myself giving him the same spiel the

Homies hit me with in my job parking lot, except he wasn't buying it. "Bruh, I'm about to be making like $300 a day, waking up when I want, keeping it lit, going on shopping sprees." I said holding up a finger for every point. "We about to take this shit from Daygo to the Bay. Then we gone hit the East Coast. Shit, the way I see it, I'm about to be balling." "Yeah, okay." He uttered in disbelief, handing me the half full bottle of Hen.

Chapter 3: From CA to GA

He picked up the two 25-pound dumbbells that was laying in the grass. He started to curl them one by one. "Well, man, just be safe out there and keep your head on the swivel. Shit, you know this summer I'm moving to Atlanta. Me and wifey got a four bedroom out there in Stone Mountain."

plug, we would fill up a U-Haul truck with boxes of books and electronics to be driven back to LA. We never did take it state to state as planned.

MONTY & L.A. LAKERS CHEER LEADERZ ←

FROM LEFT 2 RIGHT

CLIFTON POWELL
MONTY (middle)
ANTWON TANNER (white)

CLUB PORTRY
Las Vegas

Chapter 3: From CA to GA

He threw the dumbbells in the grass, plus they squeezin niggas out. This muthafucka is about to be gentrified. I didn't even know what that meant at the time. He said, "Niggas ain't going to be able to afford to live here. Man, these are going to be million dollar houses, mark my word. And on top of that, in the South, you get way more property for your money. I'm just saying, Monty, niggas ain't getting no younger. You ever want to come out there, let me know." "Good looking, Brody." We shook hands with a solid handshake. "I'm going to keep that in mind." "Shit, you never know, man. I might have to come by a house next door to you or something." "All right, old man, come on, let's smoke one and then I'll drop you off at your grandma's."

We rolled up a Peach Optimo and smoked it to a doobie. "All right, come on, let's bounce. I need to get home and feed these dogs and get ready for work tomorrow." We jumped in the blue Honda Accord. Slamming the door, the Homie whipped out the black 45 and set it on his lap, turned up the E40 and took me to the gates. "All right, Bro, don't forget what I said." "Much love, my nigga." We shook hands.

Chapter 3: From CA to GA

I hopped off the whip that I would eventually drive to Georgia. I slid in my grandma's house and watched TV until I crashed out. Within one week of moving to LA to become a full-time salesman, I immediately knew I fucked up. It was nothing like I imagined, or nothing like how they pitched it to me. Reality had set in.

I took for granted that my job at QRS Services was laid back and easy money. I sat in a chair, drinking coffee, and talking on the phone all day. Something I can do hungover, half-sleep, etc. But this here, this was a whole different grind and hustle: being on your feet in dress shoes for eight hours a day, in button-downs, with the Cali sun burning you up.

We would go to shopping plazas, walk in barber shops, hair salons, restaurants, gas station parking lots, whatever. If a place had people there, we were in it. We didn't let anybody walk past without us shooting our spiel.

Aside from being stuck in LA traffic and getting banged on everywhere we went, I wasn't waking up whenever I wanted to. We would wake up every morning between 7:30 and 8:00, no matter what we did the night before.

The Homies had a storage unit that was the headquarters of the operation. Our first few weeks out there, we stayed at the Seabreeze Motel in Inglewood, not too far from LAX Airport. The sheriffs actually raided our room one night, thinking we were doing illegal activity only to find books and electronics. The Homie Sean ended up going to jail that night. He spent the night in the LA County Jail and ended up bailing out the next day. We had weed on us and he also had some Xanax pills with no prescription.

Every day, we would round up at the storage unit and we would load the trunks with the little remote-controlled cars, the children's books, and all the other gadgets that we would sell for between $5 and $20. It was me, Sean, Trav Action, and Johnny Castro. We would rotate, working in teams of two. Some days I rode with Johnny, some days I rode with Sean or Trav, and vice versa.

We had two different whips that we worked out of, Johnny's Silver Beamer and Trav's Burgundy Thunderbird or his T-Bird from the 90s. Another small detail that these niggas forgot to mention is I would be sleeping on the couch or sometimes on the floor with one blanket and a pillow. I did this for the duration of my stay. Sometimes we would have to sleep in the car or a cheap hotel, depending on if Trav's cousin had some pussy lined up.

He was letting us crash at his house not too far from USC. He had a two-bedroom duplex. He was a funny dude. He had porno DVDs all around the house, incense burning, weed trays, magazines. The spot was draped with black leather couches: a TV, a DVD player, and minimally decorated just like a true bachelor pad. He would come in the living room rubbing his stomach with a wife beater on and say, "What y'all fools got going on tonight?" Shit, we would say watching TV with sore feet. We already knew what was coming. "I hate to do it to y'all, but y'all gotta find somewhere to crash tonight. I got some pussy coming through. Y'all straight right now. You ain't got to bounce yet. She'll be here around 10."

Then he would make small talk before casually walking back to his room. We tried not to get hotels because it would cut into the money we made for the day. We still had to buy food every day, coffee, had cell phone bills, buying dodo or weed, put gas in the car, swishers, beer, haircuts, toiletries, money to go to the laundromat.

Oh, did I tell you guys that we wasn't making $300 to $400 a day either? On bad days, we was making $50 to $80. On great days, we might take home about $250 and some change. But after you deduct all the above expenses, money was tight.

I had a lot of fun living in L.A. It also helped make a man out of me. I wasn't living with my girl or living with Granny. I was out on my own. Me and the Homies, going out, getting money every day. On the nights that we would have to sleep in the car, we would hit the liquor store, grab a bottle, get hella drunk, walk around Hollywood hollerin at females, drive around L.A., hit a club, whatever. Pretty much just killing time until we got tired enough to pass out in the car. Living in L.A. and getting up every morning to go sell merch face to face helped take my hustle and talk off to a whole nother level.

See, when I had my 9 to 5, I got a check no matter what, rather I was performing or slacking off doing half-assed work. But when you work in commission, there is no comfort or security from a guaranteed paycheck. There's no safety net. You only eat what you kill. It forces you to hustle. If I don't sell a book or a gadget, I don't have no money to eat. It forces you to grind in a different mode, in a different element. I need someone to spend this Ten with me to cover my expenses. With that kind of pressure, it breeds a certain kind of hunger, and it gives you a shark-like mentality. No sale, no money!

It will have you shooting your spiel at everyone, and I mean everyone you come in contact with. No matter the race, how old, young, dressed bummy, dressed in designer, whatever, everybody is a potential sale. We go into it knowing that you gotta get ten no's just to get one yes. So therefore, we can't afford to let no one pass us by.

The Homie Sean was the brains of the operation. Trav and Johnny had a bag and invested. Sean was tall with green eyes, and could sell rain to a cloud. He also had charisma and was a smooth talker. We been homies since Lewis Middle School days. He had the connect on the cheap merchandise, and he had quit his job to work for himself.

After being a top salesman at a company for years, he had a team of young salesmen under him that he trained. He was a GM the whole nine yards. He had this shit down to a science. He was the one that trained Trav, Johnny, and eventually me. I learned not to waste time with non-payers, just like in collections. If somebody didn't want what we were selling, dart away from them in a flash. Before they could finish saying no thank you, we would already be talking to the next customer.

In the beginning, I used to think it was rude to just walk off on people. They wouldn't be interested, they would be trying to politely turn me down, and I would be awkwardly standing there making small talk before I walked off. Telling everyone to have a good day and all that kind of shit. Not the Homies though. As soon as they could detect that you weren't buying, they damn near ran away from you to get to the next person. Getting told no over and over after being out there for hours in the blazing sun- sweating, with a handful of toys and $10 bucks in your pocket, that'll make you scramble.

I came to understand why they moved like that. In less than a week, my attitude changed and I was doing the same as them. We forged a brotherhood out there, made money together, clubbed, partied in Hollywood, Shopped on Rodeo and different swap meets, went to Venice Beach on Sundays, ate at M&M's Soul Food, Tam's Chili Cheese Fries, Smashed and dated some cool little breezys, and went to lowrider shows. It was a dope experience.

Once maybe twice a month, we would hop on that 5 South and take that two-hour ride back to Daygo to see our families and the homies. We also had to go to the warehouse in San Ysidro to restock on Merchandise. After cashing out the Merch plug, we would fill up a U-Haul truck with boxes of books and electronics to be driven back to LA. We never did take it state to state as planned.

Chapter 3: From C.A. to G.A.

We just hammered Daygo to L.A. and everything in between. Oceanside, the I.E. (Inland Empire), Temecula, Hemet, Mo-Val (Moreno Valley), Apple Valley, The L.B.C (Long Beach), etc. We were going strong for about seven to eight months before we tapped out of the game. It wasn't due to a Fallout or nothing bad happened that caused us to stop the operation. I just think we were all worn out, a little homesick and ready to do something new. Besides, I wanted to get back to making music. Plus, I was ready to jump to another collection gig and get to these bonus checks. We moved back to Daygo and I was right back in the southeast, living with my grandparents and unemployed.

I didn't even have my suitcase all the way into the house yet, before my grandpops was asking me, "what's your plans, son?" And hitting me with you need to be doing something productive talk off. Although I didn't feel like hearing his spiel right now. He had a point. I only had a little less than four grand to my name. With all my habits and life expenses, that money will be gone within a month or two. I did have a car. I managed to hustle up and get a black BMW 745 I from the auction. I'll never forget, I was still living in L.A. and my grandma called me in the middle of the night. Her first words were "Don't be mad o.k.!" I didn't even have the car a full two weeks before it ended up in car prison (the impound) The police towed it away, after they pulled over my little cousin A.C. joyriding down El Cajon Blvd at like 1:00 in the morning. This nigga found the spare key in my room. Not only was he fifteen with no drivers license but the car didn't have any insurance or registration. I couldn't catch a break. Anyways, I had a few boxes of merch and a few hundred CDs of my album The Arrival. The only problem with that is, everybody is on the mp3 players and the iPods now. C.D.'s were on their last leg. I gotta make somethin shake!

One day I was in my room with my notepad open, listening to a CD I found that had some instrumentals on it. When the homie tapped on my window. He signaled for me to come outside. I did that. We dapped up and he handed me the blunt. What's up Blood? He said, with an it's good to see you facial expression. We hadn't seen each other in almost a Year. "I'm smooth Bro, In here writing some bars."

Oh, so you in there. writing some trash Huh. Ha ha ha ha. Bursting out in laughter at his own joke.

"Yeah, trash just like that Fam Bam swap meet outfit you sporting. What it do?" "Nothing, Boolin, I was just sliding through and I saw your car; just seeing what's happening with you. I aint seen you in a little minute." He said while scanning every car that passed by. "Aww, I'm just holding on like a loose tooth homie, trying to find a job." I need to sell the rest of this merch and try to get some money up. The homie rebuttaled bro, you don't gotta sell kid toys out here. "If you want to get back in the game, I'll fuck with you. My mind started racing thinking about all the fast money I could make. He continued his talk off. You need to stop playing with the game homie and come get some real money." He continued

"Like Young Jeezy said, trappin aint dead these niggas just scared. Ha Ha." I listened intensely, rubbing my chin, looking like I was in deep thought. I didn't say anything. "Matter of fact, come with me to the car real quick homie. I'm bout to bop anyway." He hopped in his car and grabbed the backpack that was sitting in the back seat, and began to comb through it." What you trying to do?" He magically appeared with a medicine bottle full of colorful ecstasy pills and shook the bottle up. I hopped on the passenger seat. Stuffing the medicine bottle back in the backpack, He reappeared with a freezer bag full of fluffy light green nuggets with red hairs. Whats up Nigga? Talk to me, he said. And for his last trick, He pulled out a Ziploc bag full of a baby powder looking substance. "What's up, What you trying to do?" I ain't got all day. You got a G($1,000) on you? better yet... Shoot me like four-five hundred, I'll plug you in with a nice little Party Pack! Help you get right back on your feet." My heart started beating fast. Before I could respond, my grandpa yelled "Monty, come on son, it's time to eat! Get in here" He walked outside and stood on the porch. He crashed the party.

It's almost as if Allah sent him out there or something. The homie hurried up and put the party favors in the Jansport." Alright bro, I'm bout to dip." He uttered like Grandpops just blew his sale. "Aight, Hit me later." I spoke. He replied, "Oh yeah, you know D is having his going away kickback this weekend. You know ya boy is moving to Georgia." "Oh shit. Yeah, I remember. Ima be in the building!" "Alright bro, in a minute!" The homie skirted off into the dusk. I walked into the house to go eat. While watching Jeopardy with my grandparents. I was in deep thought. Contemplating if I should start back hustling again. The homies' words echoed in my head. "You need to stop playing with the game and come get some real money". I couldn't unhear it.

Fast forward to Sunday, Derrick and his wife hosted their going away kickback. In True California fashion, they barbecued in their backyard and invited family, the true homies, and the true home girls. It was children jumping and flipping in the bounce house. Lots of laughter, Talking, Music playing, dominoes and cards being slammed on the table. Shot glasses being filled up and fat blunts in rotation. After mingling for a few hours and participating in all the family fun games and activities. Me Derrick and a pack of the homies snuck away from the women, children, and older folks. So, we can chop it up unfiltered amongst the fellas. We tiptoed into his garage and pulled up a chair, on the most comfortable thing we could find.

"Ay..crack that garage, it's hot as a motherfucka in here" one of the homies said. "I got you bro" D yanked the garage door up. We started rolling up and passing around the Fifth of Remy Martin VSOP. Conversations were slow to pick up. Even though we were having fun, we were kind of sad that the homie was moving out of state. To break the silence, I asked "So you're outta here next week Huh?" "Yup, Derrick said. The moving truck will be here in a few days to pick up and pack up our furniture and shit. Then they gone meet us in Georgia to unload it at the new spot." Everybody was listening closely. "Me, wifey and my cousins are going to drive the cars out there. I responded "Damn, you ain't playin. You for real, for real moving." Somebody to the left of me said "Ay, this nigga gone come back a country bumpkin!" The room erupted in laughter. "Yeah, whatever buster ass nigga! I bet I'll knock you out though!" D, responded in a combative tone. They cut their eyes. I intervened. "How long is it gone take y'all to get there?"

"Well, we gone try to make it in a day and some change. We plan on driving non-stop! Me, wifey and my cousins are going to keep rotating the wheel until we get there. We might stop in Texas to sleep and shower. It could take two, maybe three days, depending on how long you stop for rest. "Shit Texas is so big, it takes a whole day to get through by itself. We jumping on that 10 East and we outta here homie."

Chapter 3: From CA to GA

"Ooohhh, You lucky, I gotta get out there to see you one time. I'm trying to hit Magic City!" Said a voice excitedly from the corner of the garage. Another homie interrupted and let the cat out the bag. "I heard the Cha Cha's out there is bad and they hella thick too" We all agreed, and the conversations began to get divided up between the homies. I stood up and pulled a bag of shrooms or magic mushrooms out the pocket of my Ed Hardy jeans. I announced "Might as well get it in one last time!" Everyone's eyes lit up and they began to cheer me on "Let's gettt IT!", "Ayy, slide me one!" "Hell yeah!", "Yeah Dat!", different voices began to shout out. The bag made its way around the room until we all had a mushroom cap in hand. Let's send the homie off right. We're gonna miss you, bro bro.

We chewed up the shrooms. It felt like we were in a dream, between the floating, hallucinating and feeling animated sensation. We spent the rest of the night cracking jokes, reminiscing on our teenage years and trading old war stories. The evening before Derrick and his fam were set to move, his cousin who agreed to help drive had aborted the mission. Derrick called a few other people to substitute, but no one could help drive across the country at last minute notice.

The Homie began to panic, as he was one driver short, and his wife hated driving long distances. Also, his other cousin couldn't drive across the country by herself. My phone rang. "Hello".... "Bro, what you doing?" "Posted, what it do?" It was Derrick. "Man, I really need you homie!" He sounded stressed out. "Why? what happened?" "I need you to help me move to Atlanta. We're supposed to be taken off tomorrow, at like five in the morning; And I ain't got nobody to help me get Wifey's car out there. The relly flaked out on me, and you're the only one I could rely on." He sighed... For me, it was a no brainer. I was an unemployed lost soul, and it was a two for one special. Help the homie move and get a free trip to Georgia. I was in! I spoke into the flip phone... "It's nothing, I got you Homie!" "Man... I really appreciate you Monty!"

Debt, Guns, and Dope

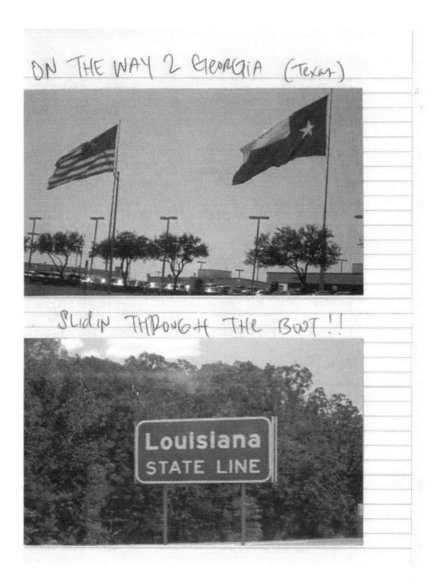

CH: 4 TOP GUN CLOSER
(DA BONUS CHECK)

M2D DAVENPORT

CHAPTER 4
TOP GUN COLLECTOR (DA BONUS CHECK)

In the dope game, the plug has love for very few people. If any at all. One person that he has love for is his top salesman/earner. The hustler that outworks his colleagues and makes him the most paper. The one who sells the most product, undetected by law enforcement. The one moving that work, faster and more efficient than anybody else hustling for him. Especially, if he's bringing back that money on time, every time and not coming up $1 Short. And for the top gun Dealer, that's not working on consignment- cashing out that work up front. He definitely loves them! To show appreciation, the plug might come to his defense as an ally in a street war. Offer him different deals on the drugs/work. Have someone bail him out of jail if he gets jammed up. He may be rewarded with a new watch, chain, or car. Depending on the level of the operation and his boss's generosity.

Well in Debt collections, the Top Gun Collector is the equivalent to the kingpins top earner or highest salesman. The agent that's making the boss the most money, by closing the most deals or getting the most payments. The hustler who liquidates the debt portfolio at the highest rate. Making the most out of each account. Hitting said budget every single month, and out collecting his or her peers in the office, or offices if the agency owner has multiple trap houses or locations.

The top gun collectors are the closers in the office. The big dogs, the budget hitters. These are the guys you go get when you're out of rebuttals, about to lose the customer, and can't convince them to pay their bill. They are the heavy hitters that come take the second Talk Off and get the payment out of the debtor. They don't take no for an answer. It's like magic how they turn non-payers into customers gladly reading their credit card number over the phone. Guys Like J.T. in the movie "Boiler Room."

These guys got an answer for everything. If you tell the closer one reason why you don't need their product or services, or why you can't pay your bill. They have three to four reasons why you do need it, while making it sound urgent and convincing.

If you tell a closer or a collector, why you can't afford to pay your bill. They then become your financial adviser, and proceed to tell you how you can tap your resources, budget, and move money around to get the bill paid. Never mind the fact that the guy telling you this is making less than $20 an hour and is probably behind on his own bills. But you gotta give them credit though! Pun intended......

"Let me get $60 dollars on pump one, two packs of black and milds, uhm... these Red Bulls, and that'll be it." The woman cashier replied, "Okay baby, that will be $92 and" ..." wait hold up. Matter of fact...and let me get five of those five-hour energy shots". Said Derrick to the attendant in the Louisiana gas station.

"Oh shit, they got catfish in the gas station out here!" I shouted out in shock. Looking down at the soul food, inside the glass case laid out buffet style.

"I'm bout to grab me a few pieces!" I said rubbing my chin. "Shit, I might have to do the combo! this food is smellin magically delicious homie" Derrick placed his bid. "Grab me a few pieces too" he said, walking out of the gas station into the muggy Louisiana heat. Until this day, that was still some of the best catfish I ever had in my life. After gassing up both cars, we jumped back on the highway heading east toward Georgia. We were almost there. After dipping through the Mississippi and Alabama, we finally saw the sign we've been looking for. "Welcome to Georgia (The Peach State)"

My phone vibrated in my pocket.

I pulled it out and flipped it open. "Yo!" …"Ay, we go get off on Wesley Chapel Rd, and stop at Mickey D's. My pops said it's right there when you get off the exit. We can't miss it."

"Aight bet" I flipped the phone closed.

We pulled into the parking lot of the McDonald's, off Wesley Chapel Rd. We stretched and celebrated that we finally made it. For dinner we copped a medley of cheeseburgers, chicken nuggets, French fries, and then we took it to the homies' new humble abode. One by one we pulled into the driveway of, A Four Bedroom home, nestled in trees with a two car garage. It was all white, with red trim and bricks neatly and strategically scattered throughout the house's frame. It was draped with a huge backyard, and a fire pit sitting on the wooden deck. Quiet as kept, I believe the homie was sitting on a few acres of land.

For the record, it was never part of the plan for me to live in Georgia. My job was just to help the homie transport his wife's car, help unload the moving truck, hang out for a week or two, and then get flown back to Daygo. Amid my second week, I immediately knew that I loved Georgia. Between the nightlife, the trees, the peaceful environment, and it being a black metropolis/ black Hollywood, I was mesmerized! I saw black cops, black bus drivers, and when going into a fast-food joint I was greeted by black, cashiers, cooks, and waitresses.

If sliding down the 285 freeway, and you spotted a Bentley, Maserati, Porsche, Mercedes, or Range Rover. It was usually a black man or woman gripping the steering wheel. My spirit felt at home, and I felt at peace. It's kind of crazy, I was experiencing culture shock in a positive way. See, where I'm from "San Diego", the black population is less than 10%. That's with the majority of black people being contained in the southeast. I love my city, but It's safe to say we are outnumbered by Whites, Hispanics and Asians. For the first time in my life, I was witnessing brothas and sistas in positions of power! Black excellence was exuberant everywhere I turned. I couldn't help but marvel at all the successful politicians, rappers, teachers, actors, athletes and entrepreneurs. Don't forget the ballers who got their riches out on the streets. Not to mention, all the Gorgeous black women of different hues, with southern hospitality and curvaceous bodies of Goddesses. Oh my God! The culture, the music, the soul food, the rich civil rights history, and a more laid-back life, that was more affordable than Cali. I really wanted to live here. Experiencing Atlanta gave me the inspiration and the spark that I too can be successful. I could smell the new opportunities in the air. Plus, I needed a change of atmosphere.

Me, Derrick and his wife Neish were leaving Stonecrest mall, after eating and doing a little shopping. On the way back to their home, I was sitting in the backseat looking out the window. Taking in the scenery with all trees, feeling the ATL vibes, and the good warm energy that the South had to offer. While driving, Derrick looked in the rearview mirror and said "Ay, I got a deposit dropping Thursday morning. Ima go ahead and book you a ticket back to the soil, I appreciate you my nig!" I was hesitant, but my gut told me to man up and just ask. I began my spiel "Dang, bro... You think I can live out here with yaw? Aint nothin poppin for a nigga back home.." He paused and glanced over at Neish. " What you think babe? Should we let this nigga stay out here wit us?.." She locked eyes with him through her Chanel sunglasses, "I'm cool with it, why not."

The homie kept his eyes on the road. "Aight, you can stay Gee, but you got nine months to find a job, get a spot and get some shit crackin" God answered my prayers. I was finally on a clean slate. At least I thought so. Now, I just gotta find a job. I jumped on craigslist.com to find a gig. My first month in Georgia, I did all types of odd jobs. I sold meat packages door to door for commission, I did odd construction jobs with the homies father-in-law, I mowed lawns, so on and so forth.

Then the light bulb went off. I needed to go back to my bread and butter. From that moment on, I filtered my job search to Debt Collections jobs. During my search, I stumbled across an ad that read "Immediate hire for an experienced Collections Representative, starting off at $300 a week salary, plus bonuses and 25% commission." That was right up my alley.

I emailed my resume to the email address that was on the screen in purple font. The next morning, I placed a follow up call to the (404) number from the Craigslist ad. I figured, let me call and check on the status of my application and possibly talk myself into a job over the phone. I opened my phone and dialed, ring ring. Georgia Financial Services please hold. They kept me on hold for a few minutes. I sat patiently, listening to the elevator music. A woman answered, "G.F.S how may I direct your call?"."Umm, yes my name is Lamont Davenport, I was just calling to check on the status of my application." I said professionally. "Okay, one moment". She put me back on hold.

After about 45 seconds, she came back to the phone. "Okay, I see yo resume here!". Can you be here tomorrow at about 1:00, for an interview? "I sure can." "Alright, Mr. Davenport, I got you all set here. Do you got the address?" "Yes, ma'am,

I see it here on the ad." In a sweet southern accent, she replied "Okay, we will see you tomorrow at one, ask for Tricia okay." "Ok Awesome! Thank you" "Bye".

After hanging up the phone, I told Derrick, "Bro, I got a job interview tomorrow" "Good shit! homie, doing what?" I continued "Collections, Ay, you think, you could shoot me downtown tomorrow?" Little did I know that the city of Atlanta was about 45 minutes west of Stone Mountain with traffic. He agreed to take me. He didn't know either. The job was in the Urban Suburban building off Martin Luther King Jr drive on the westside of Atlanta. The next morning, D dropped me off in front of the building that was erected directly across the street from a cemetery. I walked into the building and got off the elevator on the second floor. I immediately noticed that this office had a vibe to it. It wasn't quiet office chatter or playing classical or jazz music.

They had trap music and r &b playing softly in the background. The radio Played DJ Greg Street and The Steve Harvey morning show. People were cracking jokes, roasting each other. The collectors were dressed fresh with swag, like they were headed to happy hour after work. It wasn't a business casual dress code. I met with the owners, Chance, and Tricia. They were an African American couple in their early forties, who met at a collection agency that they used to manage together. They fell in love, got married and went into business together.

Chance shook my hand and said, "Davenport?... Come on, follow me this way" I trailed him into his office located in the very back. He closed the door behind us. Chance was a tall dude. Similar to the owner of QRS services. He stood about 6 '7, maybe 6' 8. He rocked a bald head with a goatee and smooth dark brown skin. He looked like money, and stayed dipped with the latest Gucci, Polo and Lacoste, coupled with the latest/ hottest new sneakers out on the market. Tricia was beautiful. She graced an almond complexion, with long black natural hair. She was always dressed stunning, with diamond studded accessories. She stayed dipped in Chanel, Prada, YSL and all sorts of expensive looking dresses and heels. She was about 5 '9, busty, humble, and smiled with pearly white teeth. She spoke with class and elegance. It seemed like every other month they were pulling a new foreign car into the park and lot. After looking over my resume, asking me a few questions about my collections experience, and gauging my personality and ability to think and answer quickly on my feet. He said "Your resume looks good. When can you start?"

"Man, I can start tonight." He chuckled. "Ok, ok I like your intensity. Can you start tomorrow?" "Yes sir" "Good deal, be here tomorrow at 10am. I'm gonna start you off at $13 an hour. Every six months, we do reviews for raises. As long as you're performing, you can make some good money here. We have a pretty laid back culture, Uhm..we have a nice bonus structure. Let me see.. What else, Oh yeah, everyday we run a contest, where you can take home cold hard cash too. I take care of my collectors. We are like a family around here." He leaned back in the Black leather chair. "Do you have any questions?" "Naw, not at the moment, I'm just ready to hammer these phones!" "Ok cool, cool. Well, we're good here. Welcome to the team man. He reached out the large guerilla sized palm for a handshake. We firmly shook hands. "Make sure you bring your ID and a copy of your social security card tomorrow. We'll need copies of those "

I belled out of the interview, feeling a sense of relief and feeling proud of myself for landing a job in a different state. While walking out of the office, I heard somebody in a cubicle saying, "All right Sir, if you don't want to pay, that's your right as an American citizen. I can't force you to pay…But hey, do me a favor, look out the window, you see that black car parked out there?" He paused…. I walked out of the office toward the elevator. I didn't think anything of it. I called the homie to have him scoop me up. I also wanted to deliver him some news that he can use. "I landed the job." He replied, "That's what's up my nig" he continued "Shit. I gotta be honest with you though... Man, this is kind of far to be driving back and forth every day, this shit's like a 40-minute dip. I mean, I can get you here and pick you up for the first week. But, after that you go have to get on the train dawg." The following morning, he dropped me off in front of the Urban Suburban building so I could embark on my new collection journey.

After being there for about an hour, I went through all the formalities. You know, take a tour of the office, meet the team leads and managers. Also, meet and introduce myself to my soon to be co-workers. I completed the rest of the application, and they ran off a copy of my California ID and social security card.

Within 10 minutes of being on the floor, I saw and heard that this was a whole new world that I never knew existed. Granted, I had only worked one collection job prior to this one. However, I was coming from a compliant collection agency. An agency that did not violate the F.D.C.P.A by any means. Meaning they did not threaten a debtor, with any repercussion that they couldn't deliver on. They also never misrepresented themselves, which is a high level F.D.C.P.A. violation. If you are a collection representative, you can't call a debtor and identify yourself as an attorney, police officer or an agent of the courts. That's considered a deceptive act or practice. In my three-week training at QRS services, I was taught about the U.D.A.A.P violation (unfair, deceptive, abusive, acts or practices.) along with the other violations.

But in this muthafucka, this was like the wild, wild west of debt collections. The outlaw debt collectors that have gone rogue. Getting money by any means. Rather they gotta tell you they're gonna garnish your wages, file a lawsuit, repo your car or put a warrant out for your arrest. These niggas was raw and uncut!

After completing my first day at G.F.S, I immediately found a new zest for debt collections. Derrick held up to his end of the bargain. He got me back and forth to work for the first week. But after that, I was on my own. Every morning, I took about a two-hour commute to work. I walked fifteen minutes to the bus stop to catch the bus heading to Indian Creek train station. From Indian Creek station, I took a 30+ minute train ride westbound to Westlake train station. Which was like a 10-minute drive or 25-minute walk from my job. Some days

I would catch the 3-bus going down M.L.K Dr to work, and some days I would just walk. I must say, working at G.F.S was like being in collections boot camp. It was straight serious business. If you didn't have a payment on the board by lunchtime you were getting sent home (without pay). Luckily for me, I had already gone through sales bootcamp in L.A., which had equipped me with a sense of urgency and a closer's mindset. I would always see people getting that tap on the shoulder and told to go home for the day because they failed to produce results. They was not playing at G.F.S. No one was given an opportunity to ride the clock or pimp the clock as we say in the biz. Chance had a Barack Obama speech pattern and vocabulary, infused with a guidance counselors' tone. He used those ingredients to create an ice cold talk off. He spoke low and slow. Forcing the debtor to listen closely to his spiel. This was done intentionally.

He had mastered the art of verbally painting the picture. He's the one that taught me how to paint the picture. Making the call come alive! Making the debtor clearly see the repercussions in their head; of what could happen if they refused to pay. He would verbally hold their hand and walk them through the payment arrangement. Encouraging them to pay and making them feel proud to have done so. Also, he was part of the elite group of closers who started off in a cubicle. He treated listening to recorded calls, like a coach treated watching and studying game footage with this team. That's one thing that we didn't do at QRS services. We would listen to recordings of other agents' calls/ Talk Off, at least a few times a week for about an hour out of the day.

All the collectors would pull up a chair, and we would be huddled around Chance with a live call blasting out of the computer speakers. He was like our captain preparing us for battle. With notepads in hand, it was mandatory that we jotted notes to the sound of the recorded conversation or the occasional live call. He would pause the recording and say, "Now what did this agent do wrong? How did they fumble the call?" After all the volunteers raised their hands and gave their best answer and input, he would calmly say "I want you to write this down" and then slide us the best rebuttal or a different direction (approach) that we could have taken on that call. I gotta be honest, Chance and Tricia really whipped me into shape as a collector. It didn't take long for me to recognize who was the Top Gun closer in the office and who were the boss's favorites.

The Top collector in the office was Bear. I witnessed everything he said, being hilarious to Chance and Trisha.

They would let each other borrow blue ray DVDs, they would pick him up for work and drop him off at home although his house was the opposite direction of where they were headed. They loaned him money against his check! All types of shit. I can recall one incident where he ended up going to jail and they bailed him out the next day. He had it made in the office. People called him Bear, not because he was big or anything but because ya' boy acted like the Chicago Bears was God's gift to football. Da Bears.

He was a B.D. (Black Disciple) from Chicago, who moved to Atlanta a year or so before I got there. Nigga was always saying "On King Dave!" Dude was a hazel eyed, fast talker that was funny, hyper, and a hell of a collector! A real player too if I must say so myself. He was smashing most of the breezy's in the office. We used to place our bid on the new, pretty little honey dips in the training class before they hit the floor. Lol. We used to take em down in the bathroom upstairs on the fifth floor, which had nothing but abandoned offices. We were some wild boys! He was my first friend in the A.T.L, the first person to take me out clubbing, show me around the city, so on and so forth.

Before becoming homies, I would be clocking out, and I would ask " What you got pop locking Bear?" "Nothin man, bout to get some wings and take my ass home to work on this talk off" "I feel you Brodie!" I would say convincingly, but I was lying. The truth is, I was winging it with my Fast talking Gift of Gab, my proper California accent and colorful vocabulary. Along with bits and pieces of the script that I vaguely remembered from QRS services. I didn't feel the need to practice. I was getting a check every Friday. I was straight (contempt). I can't lie though I was fiending for a Bonus Check. I wanted one badly. It's not like I wasn't trying, I just couldn't hit the mark. I wasn't collecting enough payments in a month. If I was setting up enough payment arrangements, the amounts I was negotiating weren't tallying to up 10k at the end of the month. Bonus checks are paid out the second pay period of every month. This is to ensure that agency owners aren't paying out bonus money on payments that declined or charged back. See, in the world of debt collections, it's all about the bonus check. If you just want the hourly pay, agency owners can detect that, and they despise it. They look at it like, you're just doing the bare minimum. "If you just want an hourly check, you are in the wrong business! Clock out, and go get yourself a customer service job!" You can hear that, being shouted on the floor of any collection agency worldwide.

The law of attraction showed me her beautiful face one afternoon. I was posted up at the Sunrise Cafe, on the first floor, on my lunch break. It just so happens that, Bear was getting off the elevator with two female co-workers. He spotted me through the window of the Afrocentric Cafe, which was the watering hole where the closers hung out, and got their coffee and grub. He threw his hands up at me "Cali, what you got goin on man? He lowered his tone. "You smoke?" "Hell yeah homie" I excitedly replied. They were on their way to smoke a blunt and get some food. We had an hour lunch break. "Come hop in wit us. We bout to go burn it down at Mozley park" "Im wit it! give me a few minutes homie, i'm waiting on my sub" "Aight, just meet us at the car" After grabbing my sub and bag of chips, I walked out the building and hopped in the backseat of the gold Ford Taurus bumping Future. On the way to A-Town Wings, Bear sparked the convo. "I be hearing you back there, getting busy on them debtors man. You got a nice Talk off" "I appreciate that homie, i'm just trying to be like you when I grow up" He chuckled, crumbling the weed, getting it ready to enter the Dutch Master. "Make a right at this light" He told the lady driving, from the passenger seat. He followed up, "Where you from man?" "Daygo, San Diego.. We about two hours south of L.A" I said, biting the turkey sub. "Thats whats up,

I'm trying to get out there on King Dave. I always wanted to go to Cali." "You'll love it out there homie. Good weed, Food, Beautiful women. Beaches and good weather. Just keep ya head on the swivel homie, and dress neutral." He was paying close attention. "Shit…quiet as kept, I been out there to yo city. I love The Chi Bro! I Flew into Midway Airport. I boogied out there with my grandparents a few years ago on Labor day weekend for a yearly Islamic Convention. We stayed at the Hyatt Regency down the street from Millenium park." "I think I heard about that before," He said. "You probably have G. Muslims fly in from all around the world to be there. They be having lectures, workshops, seminars and different shit like that. It was smooth bro. I caught the L train to the Ickey projects to get some weed and all that." Pulling into Mozley Park, he jokingly said "Man, yo ass crazy going down there. Damn, so I guess you don't want none of this pork fried rice then. Shit..I was gone offer you some too!" Me, him and the two girls started cracking up.

We got out of the car and walked to the benches in the huge grassy field. You could smell the BBQ smoke in the air. Somebody was grilling nearby. While burning it down, we exchanged some game and slang from each other's city, and discussed collections. It was at this moment, I gained access to his mentality as a Closer. He also revealed one of the main keys to his success. Practicing his Talk Off at home after work. I was hungry to know more. Roughly thirty minutes had passed by and we had smoked the blunt to ashes. The homegirl Baines said "C'mon y'all we finna be late" On the way back to work, we doused ourselves in cologne and dropped some Visine in our eyes. We casually walked back in the office like nothing ever happened, and closed out the day with a few payments each.

From that moment on, Me and Bear became homies. I was officially part of his crew. And going to work was fun. Every morning I would wake up excited to get dressed and go. To go close deals, crack jokes, flirt with the ladies and hang out with my new crew. It was me, him, a few homegirls and Moe. Moe was an incredible drummer. He had come down to Atlanta from Chicago to tour and play drums with a famous R & B singer. Between hanging out with Bear and having to take my job seriously, now that I was out of State on my own, and needed this money to pay bills and get my own place. I officially stopped playing with the game. I made a decision to dedicate my life to Debt Collections and treat it like a career. I made a vow to be the Best Closer this business has ever witnessed. My commitment and dedication was to getting big bonus checks. Nothing else mattered! I evolved to the point where I ate, slept and shitted collections.

Before meeting Bear, I would have never dreamed of doing anything work related at home. Especially not getting paid for it. He had a different way of looking at things though. He treated practicing the script, like a basketball player treated, practicing their jump shot. I credit him with giving me that work ethic. He figured, the more fluid he could deliver his Talk off and rebuttals, the more payments he would get, resulting in bigger bonus checks. He was absolutely right too. I took on his ideologies and embraced them. I started practicing my talk off at home religiously too, with anybody that would give me the time of day. My girlfriend at the time, Derrick, the neighbors, With family members over the phone. Whoever. I also used to practice with Bear at his gates. A few days out of the week, I crashed out on his couch. He lived in Southwest Atlanta in the DeerField Gardens Apt Homes.

I would catch the Marta to Oakland Train station, then catch the bus going down Campbellton Rd to get to his spot. Young Jeezy actually shouted out Campbellton Rd on one of his songs called "I Put on for my City." In one of the verses he rapped "Call me Jeezy Hamilton/flying down Campbellton" Anywho, We would Stay up all night long. Bumping music, smoking blunts, eating munchies, Snapping on eachother, taking shots, practicing the Talk Off and talking about Atlanta women and the women from our cities.

By practicing the Talk off, I mean: Role playing or doing mock calls with each other and or the mother of his child or one of the guys. It's taking turns rehearsing as the collector who's calling to close the deal, while the other person plays the hostile debtor. We also played out different scenarios of the debtor giving pushback and or refusing to pay the bill. On top of that, we would memorize the messages, the scripts(old and new),and all the rebuttals. This is something I carried on non-stop for years straight,long after Bear moved back to Chicago and we lost contact.

Chapter 4:

MONTY @ BEARS in Deerfield Gardens SW ATLANTA

WORKING ON TALK OFF

Well, my hard work and dedication had finally paid off. After a few months of practicing with Bear, I had officially become a Top Gun Collector. I was a Top Dog Closer, in the prime of his game. Easily collecting $10,000 monthly consistently. Possibly not hitting the budget in the slow months only. Which is around the holidays when people aren't paying their bills. Halloween, Thanksgiving, Christmas and New Years. I worked my way up through the ranks and had out collected every one in the office one month. I'll never forget the first time Chance congratulated me in a meeting, in front of the whole staff. While going over a report of the month's final numbers, he proudly announced "Wow..Hell of a job, Davenport. I mean you just blew it out of the water last month!" He had everybody clap it up for me.

Everyone in the office began clapping, whistling and rooting for me. "Okay I see you Davenport" "Good shit Shawty", "My Guy", different voices blurted out, giving me props. I felt proud of myself, and I low-key welled up inside receiving the praise and love of my peers. I had finally earned the respect, validation and recognition from the real Top

Gun closers. I was finally part of the Elite Group. It felt like they were welcoming me to the family. Scanning the room, I noticed that Bear and the crew were genuinely happy for me. It was no hate at all. Chance continued his speech "This man cleared almost $12,000! Shit... How long have you been here? About four months." He answered his own question and continued to hype me up. "He looking like the Lebron James of the office right now. I'm telling you, Y'all better watch out for Davenport!"

CHAPTER 4: TOP GUN CLOSER
(THE BONUS CHECK)

FOLD AND REMOVE FOLD AND REMOVE

PERSONAL AND CHECK INFORMATION
Lamont Madyen Davenport
[redacted]
San Diego, CA 92114
Soc Sec #: xxx-xx-xxxx Employee ID: 1

Pay Period: 07/07/[redacted] to 07/13/[redacted]
Check Date: 07/20/[redacted] Check #: 10045

NET PAY ALLOCATIONS

DESCRIPTION	THIS PERIOD ($)	YTD ($)
Check Amount	0.00	9793.63
Chkg 8707	415.99	4259.78
NET PAY	415.99	14853.41

EARNINGS (BONUS CHECK MONIES)

DESCRIPTION	HRS/UNITS	RATE	THIS PERIOD ($)	YTD HOURS	YTD ($)
Hourly	34.65	13.0000	450.45	886.09	10642.55
SPIFF	→				[illegible]
Total Hours	34.65			886.09	
Gross Earnings			450.45		15217.55
Total Hrs Worked	34.65				

WITHHOLDINGS

DESCRIPTION	FILING STATUS	THIS PERIOD ($)	YTD ($)
Social Security		27.93	[redacted]
Medicare		6.53	[redacted]
Fed Income Tax	S 0 No Withholding		
GA Income Tax	S 0 0 0 No		
TOTAL		34.46	1164.14

NET PAY	THIS PERIOD ($)	YTD ($)
	415.99	14853.41

Payrolls by Paychex, Inc.

0035 [redacted] 205 • Duluth GA 30096 • (404) [redacted]

MAD DAVENPORT

Every month, Me, Bear, Moe, Baines, and a cat named Mitch from Detroit, would battle head to head for the Top Collector spot. Going payment for payment, Dollar for Dollar. We would rotate the number one spot all the time. No one owned it. It was competitive and fun at the same time. The funnest part of it all though, was going to the check cashing place in the Texaco gas station to cash that Bonus Check. The Bonus Check is the collector's Christmas. Getting two paychecks in one day. Getting an additional $300 - $2000+ on top of your weekly or bi-weekly earnings. It's no better feeling. And don't let that thang come on a Friday. Can you say, balling hard? This is our one time out of the month, where we finally get to eat the sweet, juicy fruits of our labor. Not being at the mercy of bills. Having some extra paper to buy anything our heart desires. From whatever we want to eat, all the way up to buying a car. The bosses on the other hand, hate when Bonus Checks get cut on Fridays. The reason being is, collectors usually call out that Monday and or Tuesday, being to hung over to work, or just feeling like "Fuck it, I got a little money, I dont need to work." And please don't let a collector have a coke habit. He or She will get that big check on Friday. Go on a binge, and you might not see them at work again until thursday. Shit, sometimes they call out for the whole week. The bosses know what's up though. They ain't stupid. They don't get bent out of shape because they know that the collector will eventually be back to work. The bosses overstand that that little bit of money is going to run out in about a week or so. You will be right back in your cubicle with cheeks in seats, hustling hard to do it all over again. It's a never ending monthly cycle.

When I got my first Bonus Check. I dropped over five hundred bucks on a watch that I ended up losing. Me and Bear grabbed a bottle of 1800 Tequila from the package store and caught the train to Five Points. He took me to meet his Jeweler at Davinci Fine Jewelry in The Underground Mall, downtown on Peachtree. The jeweler had pictures on the wall from all the celebrities that had come into his store. I felt like a rap star that day. New Ralph Lauren Polo and Jordans on. I had a pocket full of weed and money, and I was going jewelry shopping in Downtown Atlanta. Once you get a taste of that bonus money, ain't no turning back. You are never the same. While looking down in the glass case, displaying Breitling and Rolex timepieces, Gold chains, Different color Diamonds and earrings. Big Gipp from the legendary group "Goodie Mob" strolled in, cool as a fan with no security. He had made a guest appearance, to come get his $50,000 watch repaired. Bear tapped me on the shoulder. His face lit up. "Ay, there go Big Gipp, C'mon let's go see if we can get a picture with him." Gipp handed the jeweler the expensive looking mini briefcase that held the watch. After discussing business with the Jeweler, he began to sign autographs and take pictures with all the excited fans who cheered and surrounded him.

Barging our way through the crowd. We shook his hand. "Gipp, what up! Ima big fan! They call me Monty Karlo. I'm an up and coming rapper from Daygo. It's a pleasure to meet you homie." Bear followed suit. "They call me Bear man, Chi Town!" He said "That's what's up. Yea' I fuck wit that boy Mitchy Slick outta Diego" "Yeah dat, can we get a flick wit you?

real quick" "Let's get it!" He said. He was hella down to earth, and a solid brotha. Not only did he take a picture with us, but he hung around and made small talk for a few minutes before leaving. The day just couldn't get any better.

BIG GIPP   MONTY

CH: 5
From Streets To Corporate Suites

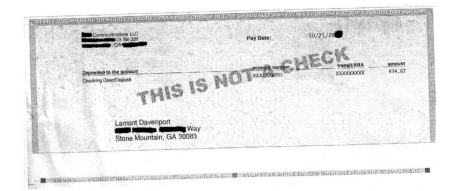

Mad Davenport

CHAPTER 5
FROM STREETS TO CORPORATE SUITES

When it comes to the dope game. Even the civilians know, one of the main goals of the dealer is to get rich or make enough money to go legit. At the very least, provide a comfortable life for him, his family, and trusted confidants. Being able to see their names tattooed on the titles of luxury cars, deeds to properties, and commercial real estate. Creating an opportunity for themselves to get out of the game and integrate into society smoothly and inconspicuously. Well, at least for the smart hustlers that's planning. In the game of Debt Collections. Agency owners share similar goals and ambitions. They just so happen to be in a different line of work, with a different approach to getting there. Although the industries and approaches differ in obtaining financial freedom. They share one thing in common. Sometimes, you must commit acts of violence to protect your Life, money, merchandise/product, and or reputation.

If you are 100% committed to the game, it is inevitable for you to meet resistance and engage in some sort of conflict, war, or battle. Someone is always gunning for your position. Attempting to pull your card and test you, to see how you react. Never forget, the opponents in your ecosystem are constantly searching for the smallest chink in your armor. Failing to handle this confrontation head on, by neutralizing the threat, can result in a lifestyle of being bullied and or extorted. One day, you will come to that fork in the road, where the game forces your hand. What are you gonna do? Fight or flight? Start going to Church or stay in these streets? Sit in prison, or snitch on your business partners, take the deal, and go home? Shoot back, or run and scream? Hurry up! You only got a split second to decide. That's literally how fast you must make a choice when you're under attack and shit is getting real!

Picture the scenery. It's Tuesday night in Atlanta, and there are very few cars out in the streets. It's almost like everybody got the memo to stay indoors except for me. The cold and heartless energy in the air was holding hands with the Georgia summer humidity. It's almost midnight, and I had just got off the bus on Campbellton Rd. I was walking to Bear's house. This is before the inception of Uber and Lyft.

Even though the streets were quiet, it still felt treacherous. Strolling past dimly lit package stores sitting in dilapidated shopping plazas and mobbing past closed gas stations and abandoned apartment buildings. Don't forget the zombie-looking drug addicts that roamed the streets pushing shopping carts. You can hear dogs barking aggressively, competing with the muffled sounds of couples arguing and cussing in the distance. The sounds of frogs and insects buzzed through the forest looking backdrop. About a block away from Bear's, I started to get the feeling that I was being trailed.

The same two shadowy figures have been walking behind me since I got off the bus. The only problem is, they weren't on the bus with me. They had appeared out of the cuts, from one of the bando's. To make sure I wasn't tripping, I jay walked and dashed across the street. What do you know, so did they.

I flipped my head around, as the footsteps got closer. Now I'm power walking. The footsteps were getting closer. "Clip-clop, Clip-clop, Clip-clop." Through the fog, I observed that the two men had hoodies on, and they were clearly bigger than me in stature. They were closing in. From behind, I heard them mumbling and semi-whispering to each other. I knew they were plotting something. But, I couldn't decode what was being said. My senses started tingling and my street instincts immediately kicked in. Suddenly, my brain flashed a warning message across the screen: "These niggas trying to rob you or something!" At this moment, I can feel them less than ten feet behind me. I picked up the pace. "Maybe I'm just paranoid. I am high." "They might just be on their way to The Deerfield apartments too. Relax Mont!" I thought, trying to console myself. But it did seem like every time I looked back, they were closer and closer.

A sketchy voice uttered "Ayy, Bruh!" I kept walking. "Yooo.. Ay Bruh, let me holla at ya." Flipping my head around to gauge how close they were. I kept it moving. Yeah I heard them, but I was ignoring them. A different voice with a deeper, more hostile tone, picked up where his comrade left off. "AY SHAWTY, let us holla at you real quick. What you got in dat backpack?" There was nothing valuable in my backpack. Just a change of clothes, pens, my notes for work, a little weed, and my phone charger. I was wearing all my jewelry though and I had a few hundred dollars on me. Their change of tone indicated that they were getting angrier, and more irritated that I was ignoring them, and disobeying their orders. Now they were jogging toward me. I still didn't respond. Ain't nothing to talk about at this time of night. Besides, they don't know me, and I don't know them. It was on! Glancing up at the crescent moon, shrouded in fog, and darkness, I began praying "God, please protect me and forgive me for what I might have to do."

In a, I'm tired of talking to you, type tone. They repeated themselves louder: "AY, BRUH. FUCK WRONG WIT U?" "YOU DON'T HEAR US TALKIN TO YO ASS?" At this point, they were getting close enough to put a hand on my shoulder. I picked up the pace. Slowly reaching under my shirt, I revealed a surprise! A Jet Black, Semi- automatic 9-millimeter pistol that I copped with one of my bonus checks. I rapidly turned around yanking the trigger. "BOOM, BOOM, BOOM!!.......BOOM!.......BOOM, BOOM!!" It sounded like a fireworks show. My ears were hissing, and my heart was about to jump out my chest! But, I had successfully ambushed them muthafuckas. They never saw it coming. The flash coming out of the barrel lit up the night sky, with every shot that I fired. I felt the power, watching them run for their lives! After the gun smoke cleared, the silhouette of a lifeless body flopped to the concrete. The body tensed up and began twitching in the pool of blood that was now forming. Until this day, I still don't know if I killed him. The incident never made the news. What I know for sure, is that I struck him twice. One bullet ripped through his neck, and I couldn't tell if the other shot hit his chest or shoulder. Before fleeing the scene, I caught a glimpse of him squirming on the ground looking like he was choking himself. He was holding the open hole in his neck, in a desperate attempt to keep blood from gushing out. He was crying like a baby, as he gasped for air and choked on his blood. He screamed with all his might, but only faint whispers came out "mama……mama…som..bo...dy"…Gasping.. "please hel…. mama."

The other assailant bolted off. Sprinting at top speed into the night's fog. "YEAH RUN….PUNK ASS NIGGA!" I roared into the night air, with a hot gun in hand. He never even looked back. I could be standing right next to him, and wouldn't know it. I never saw gods face. Before his homies body hit the concrete, he was already halfway through the woods, ducking for safety. I aint gone lie, he did bust back. I heard like two or three shots in the air, as he made his escape. It was too late though. It was already man down, and I was ghost. I darted through the dirt trail that led to the backside of the apartments. The sprint got reduced to a brisk walk. I needed to catch my breath, and stuff the 9 inside my backpack. With

Mad Davenport

my second wind on deck, I jumped the chain link fence, and began dashing through the breezeways. Finally, I made it to the staircase that held the homies apartment. I frantically banged on the door, and rang the doorbell over and over again. Ding, dong, ding, dong, ding dong!

Knock, Knock, Knock. "Ayyy….. OPEN THE FUCKIN door my nigga!" Knock, Knock, Knock. The door finally swung open. I was met by Bear standing in the doorway. He said. "Yo man, why yo lil ugly ass bangin on my?" I bulldozed past him, and forced my way into the house. He knew something was wrong. He ain't never heard me talking that fast and that aggressively. On top of that, I was sweaty and jittery from my adrenaline still pumping. Tossing my backpack on the floor, I pulled up a chair at the dining room table. "Ay, you ain't got no drank? Pour up nigga, I need a shot" "How the family doin? What's up wit ya boy Moe?" I stood up to look out the window. I just knew at any given moment, we would hear those loud bangs on the door. Followed by "This is the Atlanta Police Department" I rambled on. "I know you wasn't sleep this early. What up wit you? You ain't got no fruits (weed)? Roll up homie!" I was talking a mile a minute, falling apart with every word. I've been around plenty of guns, and shot them before. But this was my first murder. It hit different. Bear grabbed the bottle of Pinnacle Vodka that sat on top of the refrigerator and poured us up some shots. You can hear police sirens in the background and the sound of helicopter propellers. Jutting and looking at me out the corner of his eyes indicated that Bear knew what time it was, but we never spoke on it. What's understood doesn't need to be explained. We didn't even practice our talk off that night. We just played NBA 2K on Xbox, smoked and just chilled. I didn't sleep that night. As the credits roll, about almost a year later, me, Bear and Moe became the dream team of the office and worked our way up to team leaders. We got a raise and we were all given about four collectors under us that we were responsible for.

On our breaks and lunch breaks. We used to smoke in the abandoned apartment complex that was right next to our office plaza before the gentrification took place. Now their luxury condos.

One day while going to Texaco, we saw the apartment complex Luther Landings right next to our office building, leasing apartments. They had two bedrooms/ one bathroom, going for $595 a month. You couldn't beat that with a baseball bat. I figured it was the best idea to apply, especially since I was on the West side all the time anyway, and I was always catching an hour and a half train ride across town. I ended up landing an apartment at Luther's Landing. It was fun and convenient. Every morning I would wake up and take about a four minute walk to work. It was super convenient. Life was sweet! On my lunch breaks, I would go home to smoke and eat. Those were some of the funnest times of my life. Luther's Landing was my first apartment in Atlanta. The streets know them as the yellow bricks. Although, when I lived in them they were gray not yellow. But, people from "The A" know what I'm talkin bout. Right next door to the Texaco gas station, or what used to be called The Right Stuff. We would have barbecues, parties, drink, smoke, pop beans (ecstacy), play spades, tonk, and slam bones (dominoes). Coworkers would always come over after work. My apartment became the party house and hang out for the Closers. People would come through after work, and we would practice our Talk Off, order wings, pizza, Chinese food, have swinger parties and all that! The package store was right down the street. Even though it was in the hood, I loved my apartment. It was a tight knit community feeling. Everybody knew each other, shared their resources and looked out for one another. People always gave a friendly wave and spoke when I walked by. I returned the favor. Pulling in, you can always find older folks sitting on their porch in rocking chairs. As the children played and the dope boys made their money.

While living in Luther's Landing, I was right around the corner from a project called The Bluff. My girlfriend at the time introduced me to Curtis Snow, who happened to be making a movie he wrote and directed, called "Snow on the Bluff." It was one of the first films on Netflix, and ended up winning a Sundance Film Festival award. I also met somebody who hooked me up with the studio, and I got back into my music.

I pressed up a thousand CDs of "The Arrival" with my bonus check money, and began buying instrumentals or finding instrumentals wherever I could. I was back making songs. I put out a mixtape called "Karlo wit a K" because I'm killing these niggas. While trapping in the office and in the streets, I invested by pressing up five thousand CDs of "Karlo wit a K" and began selling them in the streets. I chose to use my bonus check a little more wisely, being that I fucked my other bonus checks off on clothes, shoes, jewelry, fast food, and partying.

Curtis Snow was a Stand Up nigga. Much Respect to him! I didn't know him all like that, but We did kick it occasionally in the hole on James P. before he went to serve his bid in prison. One summer weekend on the streets, me and Bear were walking around downtown during the BET Awards. It was being filmed in Atlanta that year. I ran into JT the Bigga

Figga (Hip Hop/ Independent Hustle Pioneer), while networking and passing out CDs. He had just touched down to Atlanta too. I was out selling CD's trying to make a name for myself. It was an eye opening experience. I told myself, one day, I'm going to be performing in this muthufucka.

One afternoon, I was coming home from work and saw an eviction notice on my door. I was puzzled because I was paying my rent on time every month. Come to find out, the landlord was stealing money. Collecting rent but wasn't turning in the payments to the owners of the property. As a result, my black ass was on the verge of being homeless. It all made sense though. I was wondering how this nigga stayed in all these new cars. I figured he was making decent money, but I knew the apartment complex wasn't paying that much. One day you'll see him in a new Cadillac Escalade. One day he'll be in a new Chevy. One day he would be in A BMW, and he stayed fresh on top of that. It all made sense now. After going to court and fighting it. I ended up losing, and it was right back to the East Side. I found an apartment in Kensington Station Apartments on Memorial Drive in Stone Mountain. Right across the street from Kensington train station. Getting on the train, commuting across town to the Westside every day was tiring. I started to come in late. My numbers started to slowly drop and things just weren't the same anymore. I didn't have the same spark and the same energy. Eventually. Chance and Tricia, let me go.

Although my feelings and my ego was hurt for getting fired, I had no time to pat myself on the back, or I had no time to feel bad about it. I had to lick my wounds and get back to my grind.

This rent isn't going to pay itself. I jumped back on Craigslist and saw an ad for collectors starting off at $18 an hour in Duluth, Georgia. I didn't know where it was, but I soon found out. I also found out something that was similar to San Diego and probably even across the United States. It seemed like all the good jobs are always up North. Duluth, Georgia was about 35 to 40 minutes north of where I was coming from. I found a job at WX Financial. It was run by a cat from New York named Sparkz. He was from the forgotten city, Buffalo, New York, but also grew up in Harlem. His mom was a school teacher and His pops was a gangster from the legendary 3M Nation. Do your homework. A conglomerate of three gangs. The Matadors, The Mad Dogs, and The Manhattan Lovers. Legend has it, Sparkz was a stickup kid and the mastermind of a heist back in the early nineties that netted a few hundred thousand dollars. He grew up attending private schools because his pops had real street money. He stood about six feet tall. An arrogant dude who stayed with a fresh haircut and 360 waves. Sparkz loved balling out on strip clubs, cars, and fresh gear. He was a street dude, but hella educated and had strong family values.

You've probably been to a few concerts that he funded. He brought a lot of famous rappers and R&B singers the city. But you would never know it as all he did was hang out backstage.

I later discovered he silently invested in a couple of independent movies that you probably seen on Netflix or Tubi too. I caught the train to Doraville train station and jumped on the Gwinnett Transit bus to get to the office on Satellite Boulevard. Upon walking up to the opulent building that was encased in nothing but glass windows and water fountains, I immediately saw the difference between this building and the urban suburban building on the west side. This building was the home to attorneys, insurance agencies, and other prestigious Fortune 500 companies. When I walked into the corporate suite, I shook his hand. "How are you doing, sir?" "Lamont, Davenport? Follow me this way." He said, in a heavy New York accent, "Have a seat." I closed the door behind me looking over the opulent view. I handed him a copy of my resume, scanning the resume for about 30 seconds. He tossed it on his desk. "Your resume looks good, but I see nice resumes every day, and when I get 'em in here, they can't close the door."

He wanted to do a mock talk off to test my skills. Right there on the spot. This is all I needed. He said, "Let's go ahead and roll play real quick. I'll be the debtor. You'll be the collector." "Alright, no sweat." I said "Ring, ring, ring. Hi, may I speak to Mr. Sparkz?" "Yeah, this is him. Who is this?" "Yes. Hello, Mr. Sparkz. My name is Lamont Davenport, calling from the mediation department. Is this Sparkz social ending in 1, 2, 3, 4?" "Yeah, this is him. What is this about though?" "Well, sir, the nature of my call is to inform you, I do have a two-part complaint being filed against you here. One for a breach of a legal binding contract. The second claim here is for an attempt to defraud a financial institution. It shows that you took out a loan in the amount of $1,200. Do you recall that?" "No, No.. I don't know what you're talking about!"

He said trying to knock me off my game. I turned up the heat on him. "Okay. Well, I do show here that on the application you did put down your social security number and, your banking information from Wells Fargo ending in 1, 2, 3, 4. Is this your ACH information?" "Maybe." "Okay, Sir. Well, it looks like you have to file an affidavit with the courts for identity theft because…" "Okay? Okay. Okay. Okay. I heard enough. Damn!" He rubbed his hands together. "You one of them old school heavy hitters! You nice Yo….Shit.." "Thank you!" I reminded humbly. He leaned forward in the chair and clapped. He was happy with my performance. He said "Aight. I like your style. B, when can you start?"

I hit him with my famous rebuttal. "I can start tonight." He smirked. "Okay, well, you can't start that soon, but I do have an opportunity for you. Let me just tell you a little bit about the company. We're business casual. Monday through Thursday, Friday we dress down. I do buy lunch for the office every other week. We got a pretty nice bonus structure. Come on. Lemme show you around the office. Now the starting pay is $18 an hour, but man, you an animal and with a beast like you, I'm not going to disrespect you, yo. I'll start you off at $19, all right? " "Yes, sir." I happily replied. "But you got to come in and do numbers. The budget starts off at $12,000 a month." "Man, that's small Fries to a Big Mac." He chuckled "Okay, I like your confidence. Come on, I'll show you around." Collection agencies cut straight to the chase, unlike other jobs being that they have a high turnover rate so they hire people quickly. Collection agencies are like a revolving door. People are constantly coming in and out. This business isn't for everybody. Some people have sales experience or customer service experience and come in and find out this is a totally different animal, and some of the skills that they have obtained are not helpful when it comes to the elusive debtor with an attitude.

I followed behind him as he showed me around the huge office space that housed about 30 collectors or maybe even more. "This right here, this is our P.P.A department (partial payment arrangements.) Over here. This is our Pre- Legal department. That's where im putting you." He pointed to the cubicle section over to his right. People nodded their heads and waved at me. He continued with the tour. "Alright, back here, this is our quality assurance department. They pretty much sit back here and listen to recordings all day." "Hey, Sparkz" women said in the background. "Hello. Hello! Ohh, I saw your son scored two touchdowns against LoveJoy!" He said. I noticed he had personal relationships/ connections with all his collectors. He continued, "Over here we have our human resources." I waved at the human resources lady that was sitting behind the computer. "And over here we have our bankruptcy department. So, as I was saying, we'll start you off at $19 an hour. We just ask that you come in and do your job. The hours are Monday through Thursday, 10am - 7pm. On Fridays we do 9am - 2pm. You have weekends off. The only Saturday that you work is on the last Saturday of the month" (which is closeout). Working on the last Saturday of the month for closeout is typical in the collection industry as agencies try to get all the money they can before the month ends.

While looking around the office, I purposely didn't smile. Letting people know that I'm a Top Gun collector, I mean serious business, and I'm coming for your spot. They can smell the intensity on me. "Well, that's everything. Just bring me your ID and your social, so we can run off a copy of it. We'll get you rocking and rolling, baby. I'll have your logins and everything for you tomorrow aight." "For sure. Appreciate you, bro! Thank you for the opportunity." "No doubt. All right, see you tomorrow at 10."

My first week at WX Financial, I immediately noticed that these collectors were eating high off the hog. They weren't as hungry as I was. They were living off their post dates, meaning payments scheduled to clear that they had closed previously. They would let calls from the dialer just ring and ring. Me, I was answering all those calls. Those could be potential debtors and payments. Also, they weren't going through their whole series of rebuttals. When someone told them that they couldn't pay or gave any kind of pushback, they would easily give up on the call. Okay, well, we'll call you in 30 days. Me, on the other hand, I wasn't taking no for an answer. I was fresh out of bootcamp at the pinnacle of my talk off. I was closing everything moving. The only person in there that was going as hard as I was was an old school collector. My boy, Byron. He was an old school heavy hitter collector, who was doing $20,000 a month and better. He's the one that trained me to go from doing $12,000 and $15,000 monthly, to $20,000 and beyond.

When he heard me collecting, he took a liking to me and immediately took me under his wing. We would chill together, smoke together on our lunch break, and he would tell me funny stories about his days in the army and other adventures. He knew martial arts. He jumped out of a plane before. Fought in wars. Man, this dude seemed like he did everything in life. He also was not playing with these agency owners about his money. He was the one that showed me. Sometimes you got to use a little bit of force to get your money out of these owners. Legend has it that one time somebody came up short on one of his checks, and he took the owner into the conference room, locked the door behind him. People say there was some furniture moving around and screaming. All I know is he got his money. On days where the boss brought lunch. You would hear the tone of the ungrateful collectors. "Girl, come on, I'm going to my car. I don't want that shit again. I don't want no Jersey Mikes. I'm fucking tired of sandwiches!" Me on the other hand, I was just happy to have a free lunch. I was coming from where all you got was coffee, donuts, and an occasional lunch here and there. But here they had the whole shit catered, laid out drinks, chips, sandwiches, Mexican food sometime Italian sometime, pizzas in the break room.

I say all that to say I was collecting with a different intensity. I was hungry for a bonus check, like a vampire for the blood. It was easy for me to walk them. Within 90 days of being there. Sparks immediately recognized my hustle and gave me props. He also gave me a raise. Me and Byron (B-Dizzle) became a two man tandem. The two headed monsters. We used to take each other's second talk offs. Playing good cop and bad cop, depending on the situation. Sparks loved it. He got a kick out of it. Him, the other managers and his business partners would side bet on who would get the most payments that day. I would hear 'em. "Yo, I got a hundred on Monty." "Fuck it. I got a hundred on my boy B-Dizzle." It was a good, fun, healthy competition. It helped shape the culture of the office as well.

I studied B- Dizzles Talk Off and and executed it the way that Kobe Bryant studied Michael Jordan's moves.

One day I used the classic military talk off, I got from him. He didn't know I had it in the back pocket. A rookie collector was struggling with a debtor. Getting jammed up by somebody that was in the army. He was in direct violation of the number one rule. Which is to always control the conversation. Sparkz had his door open and the office was quiet, as there weren't many people on the phone. This jackass was fumbling around with the call. The guy in the military was applying pressure, "I am in the Army. There is no way I took out this loan." "Well sir." Cutting him off "WELL SIR, NOTHING! Don't you have any respect for the men and women who serve this country? to protect your freedom." He stuttered trying to find a rebuttal. Looking like a deer in the headlights. I said "Put the call on hold, I got you Bro" He handed me the headset for a second Talk Off. I took the phone off mute. In a stern tone I began "Yes sir. My name is Lamont Davenport, one of our senior members here with the firm." I kept talking, not giving the debtor a chance to speak. He did enough talking already.

"I caught the tail end of the conversation you were having with one of my agents here. It's my understanding you took out a loan, and you're directly refusing to pay it back?" I paused. He said "As I told the last guy on the phone..How could I have taken out this loan when I'm in the military? I was stationed in Germany at the time he claims I got the loan." I returned fire instantly "Okay, sir. Was your address?"

I gave him his address. "Yes, that was my address." "Okay sir. It shows this loan was taken out two years ago. What year were you deployed? Are you sure you didn't take it out? prior to you going to serve our country?" He was losing steam, I was verbally breaking him down. He said "No, I was still making decent money at that time, and wouldn't need a loan." I sighed "Okay, Mr. Collins! If you say so, give me one second here." I put him on hold to let him sizzle.

I got back on the phone. "Alright sir. It shows here that we did send you out a validation of debt notice giving you 30 days to dispute the debt or any portion thereof. We don't have any returned mail from the postmaster general. So we know that letter was delivered successfully" I loaded up the Atomic Bomb and dropped it on his lying ass "And also, let me bring something to your attention Dave. Per Article 135, Section 7, Paragraph D of the UCMJ, it does state that you cannot have any outstanding debts. Having any outstanding debts, It clearly states you can and will be reduced in rank. Now, if you don't want to pay us sir, don't worry about it. We can terminate this call right now and I'll just contact your lieutenant." He was discombobulated "Wait, wait, wait. Hold on! Give me a second.. Wait, what year did you say this was from?" "2009 sir." "Okay, well my wife may have taken it out. I don't know. How much will it cost to just clear this shit up? I don't have time for this." I broke him down. "We can go ahead and close it out for $756.49 cents. But you must remit that balance in full today." "Alright, do you guys take check by phone?" Everyone was looking at me like I was a wizard. I magically turned an RTP (refusal to pay) to a payment in full. I heard the indistinct chatter of "Whoo" "Shawty a beast" "Oh shit!" I always got a thrill out of closing the refusals, and being the center of attention. I looked over at B-Dizzle as I wrote down the credit card number. He smirked and gave me a salute. Pun intended.

Honestly, I was just showing off, but this office was no joke. It was extremely corporate. At Least on the surface. This was the most corporate job I worked for thus far. There was no talking loudly on the floor. Also, this office was technologically advanced. We weren't using the old fashioned desk phones. We had headsets and softphones (dialpad on the computer). You could actually click the phone number and dial. No more smashing buttons. Another bonus was, this company was an aggressive dialer company. Meaning they used the automated outbound dialing system. The system called hundreds of numbers per minute, doing the calling for the agent. All we had to do was sit back and wait to hear a beep in your ear. Then boom, a debtor would be on the phone. Every now and then we would cold call, but for the most part we just took inbound calls. Another thing that I instantly noticed was, we didn't have an in-house merchant. When I was at QRS services, and the agency on the west side, we could process payments right there on the spot.

As a manager, I simply logged into the payment portal. After entering the credit card number, the debtor's first and last name, the billing address, and the amount we were processing, we got that money on the spot. The system would automatically email them a receipt and everything. But here, we used an outside merchant. Or third party merchants. Every time we obtained credit card information from a debtor, we would write it down on a payment slip and take it to the payment processing department. After charging the debtor a $12 processing fee per payment, they emailed the slip to the merchant in New York. We were trained to inform the debtor, we'll call them back within five to 10 minutes with a confirmation number if the payment is processed, or we will call them back to let 'em know if there was any discrepancy with the payment.

This was my first in-depth glimpse into merchant processors. Here is where I also learned how to track payments using an

Excel spreadsheet instead of writing them down. I was also given a company email, and held responsible for sending out the V.O.D or validation of debt letter. Also, when somebody paid off the account, I would send them out, the Paid in Full letter. This trap was very corporate. I definitely learned the structure and etiquette of a corporate agency. On the flip side, we were saying some raunchy and unsavory things to get that money. The bonus structure was sweet too, just as Sparkz promised. If you collected $12,000 (your goal), you automatically got $1,000. And, he gave you 10% of everything you collected over the $12,000. You could walk away with some fat Bonus Checks! They also had nice daily money spiffs or a daily money contest. If you got three or four green payments (cleared the same day), you automatically got $30 cash, and at the end of the week, if you were able to have 25 payments cleared, you got an additional $75. Did I mention the mid-month (middle of month) bonus too. Mid month is: if you collect half of your budget by the fifteenth of the month. That was an opportunity for another bonus, on top of your bonus check. I was knocking 'em all out of the park. I was killing it.

Another strategy I was executing that my spoiled counterparts wasn't, is I was collecting $500 a day. Or

$10,000 a month in new money. There are 20 collection days in a month not including weekends. Four weeks of Monday through Friday. I was sticking to that system and destroying it. This is the hustle and tenacity that made Sparkz love me. Along with cracking jokes and bringing good energy to the office. Everybody loved me, from the janitor to the owners (except the haters). I had successfully transitioned from the Streets to Corporate suites.

CH: 6 Party Like a Boss
(My Own Shop)

Mad Davenport

CHAPTER 6
PARTY LIKE A BOSS (MY OWN SHOP)

When working your way up in the dope game, from corner boy (selling small quantities of drugs) to kingpin Status. One of the most pivotal moments in your career is when the plug invites you to go out, or hang out with him and or the crew. When your loyalty, work ethic, and responses to pressure situations, proved that you can be trusted. You've earned an opportunity to party, and or have fun with him outside the confines of business. Blessing you with an all-access backstage pass to how the ballers move, talk, interact, and have fun. It's almost like an informal promotion. Although, it can be formal, if the plug invites you out to celebrate your moving up the ranks inside the operation. In my line of work, having the rare chance to party with your boss outside of office hours is similar. Getting a behind the scenes look at your boss drunk and or high. Letting their hair down, acting in a rare form. Being him or herself with no additives or preservatives. A whole lot of cussing and spewing their opinions, Belief systems, Political views, business principles, and ideologies unfiltered. I had collected so much money, while keeping it so real, that I reached this level of the game.

It was a normal Friday evening, after work hours. All the collectors had left the office to get their weekend started. The reason I was still hanging around, is because I trapped my way up to management, and had to finish the daily reports before leaving. The daily reports consisted of: The total amount of money the team collected that day (collectively & individually), total number of declined payments, who was tardy, absent, ect. Things were going amazing at the office. I did a hostile take over and became the Top Collector, with nobody being able to dethrone me. (Except B-Dizzle) After crushing the $15,000 monthly goal for over a year, along with helping rookie collectors and being cool with everybody. I earned a raise, a desk, and my own section of the office. I was given a crew of eight collectors to hustle under me. It was my duty to make sure that they came to work on time, and hit their monthly production goals of $12k. They also had me issue out discipline and training as needed. When and how I see fit.

Within three months of me managing my own platoon of closers. We were out collecting all the other teams in the office. I mean, just blowing them out the water. It wasn't even close. My crew was single handedly doing almost $170,000 a month, when the other four teams were barely clearing about $120.000. Aside from me being at the Zenith of my Talk Off, and closing everything moving. I took pretty good bill collectors and transformed them into Top Gun Closers. I put them through collections bootcamp, the same way that I experienced it. I prepared my soldiers for battle the same way Chance and Tricia used to prepare us. Atleast one day out of the week, I would pull them off the phones for about an hour, to listen and study calls. I encouraged them to practice their Talk Off at home, using big Bonus Checks as the motivation. I also made examples out of low performers. Showing no mercy, when making them clock out early without pay, in front of everybody. I would tap them on the shoulder and say: "Go ahead and shut your computer down, we'll see you tomorrow." Initially Sparkz was skeptical of my strategies. He used to always drag me in his office, for impromptu meetings. "Monty, I love your intensity yo, and I respect your hustle. But, you gotta relax on sending these people home for not having a payment by lunch. You're being too hard on them, son. They got families to feed, and they need they 40 hours. Do you know people saying I should fire you? They saying you're abusing your power." I shook my head, Anxious to interject. "Well, they aint grinding and collecting like they got a family to feed! They too comfy homie. They pimpin your clock!" I would respond. But the meeting would always end with me saying "I understand. My bad bro. Ima tighten up, I got you!" Only to keep repeating the same offense over and over again. I didn't give a fuck! My crew, my rules. He was just going to have to fire me. Which I knew he wasn't, Ima cash cow. Plus, once he saw how much bread my crew was generating for the operation. He started singing a different song. One day, I overheard him closing out a meeting with the other team leads and managers "And if they ass- aint got at least one payment by lunch, send em home" I was cracking up. At this moment, I've been in Atlanta a few years now, and I low-key know my way around the city. After closing out the books and logging out of the system, I emailed Sparkz the finished reports.

Tap, Tap Tap... I gently knocked on the open door. Sparkz was looking down, signing some documents on the executive cherry wood desk. His office was neat and organized with a gorgeous panoramic view of Buckhead. It sported bonsai trees, a dart board on the wall, framed pictures of his wife and kids, along with Buffalo Bills paraphernalia. I peeked my head in "Alright G, I'm about to boogie up outta here. I'll check you out on Monday, have a good weekend....Oh yeah, check your email too, I sent you the final numbers." "I appreciate that. Aight Davenport, have a good weekend son! Great job this week too." Half way out the office, Sparkz stopped me in my tracks. "Ay yo, what you got up for this weekend?" "Nothing major homie. I might grab a bottle. Probably throw somethin on the grill. Call a little breezy over or somethin. I don't know."

Translation: "Nigga im broke, and im trying to play the back burner, cus we dont get paid till next Friday and I gotta make my money stretch" I asked "Why, whats the deal? What you got poppin?"

He said "We probably gonna be making a movie at the strip club again. Yo, come party wit us my nigga. Ima show you how we do it. I think I threw like $10,000 in Blue Flame last weekend. We changed the weather in that bitch! Word up." "Damn.. You wasn't playing wit em" I replied. Trying not to sound impressed that he was spending three months of my salary in one night, on strippers and liquor.

I said "Im wit it. You got my number, just tap my line." "No doubt." Standing in front of the bus stop, my mind began playing tricks on me. "Man, he aint gone hit me up" "If he does, I aint even gone answer. Ima tell him I was balls deep in something." "Besides, I aint even got nothing to wear" "I need to do some laundry." The truth is I was making excuses. Attempting to justify why I didn't want to go. I was ignoring my insecurities about being the potential butt of all jokes for the night. Walking entertainment for the Ballers. The dude livin check to check, in a circle of rich niggas.

I could hear it now. "Man, Shut yo broke ass up. Ba, Ha, Ha, Ha" As I Stand there in Burlington Coat Factory, and South Dekalb Mall gear. While these niggas is dipped in the latest Louie, Burberry and Prada. Holding bottles of champagne with diamonds sparkling and shit.

The bus pulled up in front of me and opened its huge doors. I hopped on, tapped my breeze card, and took a seat. When I got home, I ordered a pizza and hit up one of the homies from the office. He's a team lead too. "Big Ugly…What's good with you homie? Lol." "Davenport, Wat up? Egg head ass lil boy?" We laughed together. "Chilling man. About to kill off on some pizza. Ay, tell me why Sparkz wants me to slide to the strip club with him and his homies tomorrow night" "Shit, dat sound like the move. You goin?" "Probably not bro." "What!? Why not!?" "Man, my money shorter than a dwarf on his knees right now. You know we don't get paid till Friday." "U trippin shawty. U thinkin too hard. If he askin you to come out, you aint go have to spend nothin, TRUST me! Them niggaz rich as hell bruh! If you don't wanna go, call them and tell em, I'll sub in for you." I felt where he was coming from. I chuckled. "You right bro. Fuck it, ima go turn up. Alright, let me hit you back, this my uncle Man on the other line." "Aight, Tell unc I said wat up, peace."

Fast forward to Saturday afternoon, I received a call from a (716) area code. "Monty..What up?" "Sparkz! What's pop locking wit you?" I was surprised that he actually called. "Maxin and Relaxin, about to hit the barber shop. You ready to turn up nigga? Like that old DJ Quik song, Tonight is the Night (he sang)" I started laughing. "Man, you dont know nothing about that Quik homie" "I fucks wit DJ Quik son." He said.

"Aight, you might know good music. But hell yeah, Im ready G, I just gotta hit the mall and grab a fitter." "Aight bet! What you about to cop? A Dickies suit?" He said cracking up at his own joke. Before I can get em back he kept talking. "But naw, on some serious shit. I'll be there to grab you around like nine. We gonna pre game at the Penthouse and then head out" "Hell yeah. Lets get it!" "No doubt. Uhm, text me your address. I'll hit you when i'm headed your way." After hanging up, I caught the bus to South Dekalb mall to get the freshest fit I can find with my $200 budget. Night time had crept in. After showering, and getting fresh from head to toe I was ready for showtime. I plopped on the couch, cracked open a beer and awaited Sparkz call. My Sidekick vibrated. "Yo, come outside." When I got downstairs, I saw Sparkz sitting in a bumble bee yellow Porsche Cayenne truck.

I excitedly hopped in and gave some dap. "Whoooo! This muthafucka clean bro!" Looking around nervously he said "Yea, Yea. Clean, thank You. Damn, these some raggedy ass apartments. What's these bando's? How much am I paying you L.Boogie? Shit!" I said "Come on homie, We all know you a cheapskate, let's stop with the shenanigans. Gettin a raise out of you is like pulling a tooth." We bumped fists and laughed. Cruising over uneven speed bumps and swerving around potholes, he said "You might be right. Shit, I still should of brought my heat though... Man, we go have to get you outta here son. I'm scared for your life." Looking out the window, I asked "So, what's the move? Where we goin tonight?" "Club Blaze. It's on Moreland. That's my joint right there. Thick Bad Bitches son, all types of flavors. And they food on point." His face lit up. "See, niggas sleep on Blaze Yo. Everybody always talking about Magic and fucking Blue Flame But Blaze..... Matter of fact, you'll see" I clapped my hands "Let's get it! The only Strip club I been to out here is Pin Ups." He merged lanes. "Ohh Yea, I got a few little shorties up in Pin Ups. We going to have some real fun tonight L. I'm glad you came out." "Me too homie. Real talk." Sparkz continued "My man's flew in from Jersey last night too. You gonna meet him. He a real stand up nigga. I been knowin em since da sandbox and chocolate milk, ya heard. He back at the penthouse with Josh and my other business partners. Ima introduce you to them too." "That's what's up!" I said feeling honored. "We almost there." After 30 minutes of slithering through the Atlanta traffic we arrived to the luxurious Skyscraper. Sparkz tapped his key fob and the gate began to open. We pulled into the underground parking garage.

After going up seventeen stories on the elevator. We got off and walked down the elegant five star hotel looking hallway. The door opened up to a pool table in the middle of the living room. Surrounded by expensive art, white furniture and bosses holding red plastic cups, beers and cigars. I instantly noticed I was overthinking my gear too. Nobody was even designered down like I imagined. It was a combo of Jeans, Tim boots, T-shirts, Jordans, Polo and Lacoste. All the shit I could afford. "What up son?" I heard followed by head nods.

"Cali whats up my nigga?" Said Josh (another manager from the office.) "Ayyy.. What's goody? bro bro" I began passing out handshakes and introducing myself to the unknown faces. "What's up homie. Monty" "Pleasure to meet you kid, heard a lot about you." Josh followed up. "Damn..Ya'll niggaz love some plaid dont you" The joke fell flat. He chuckled while clapping his hands. "Ay..But so does ya baby mama, she the one who brought me this shirt" The room exploded with laughs. "Oohh.. Damn L. You ain't have to do him like that son!" Josh gave me the, ok you got me look.

Sparkz homie from Jersey took the stage "Y'all ready to take some shots?" Hands began to go in the air. "For sure" "Hell yeah" "Turn up" Different voices began to sign up for a shot. After the shot glasses were filled to the brim, everyone held them up toward the ceiling fan. Sparkz looked around the room and said "This is to success fellas! I also want to congratulate my boy L.Boogie, for destroying his budget and grinding his way up to management. Salute!" We clinked the shot glasses and began chugging. I found myself daydreaming. Staring out of the floor to ceiling windows, that overlooked the Downtown Atlanta skyline. It was a breathtaking view of the city.

Looking down between the skyscrapers, I saw couples riding in the back of the horse and carriage. The view also boasted colorful lights that illuminated the sky from Centennial Olympic Park. Sparkz turned on some music and began bobbing his head to the beat. He said "Yo Monty.. It's some beer and some champagne in the fridge. Help yourself! There's some food in there too, if you're hungry." "Good looking G" I said, making my way towards the fridge. Sitting on the pool table, and smirking, Sparkz announced "Yooo, y'all niggas tryin to turn it up a notch?" He began digging in his pocket, and pulled out a bag of Sugar Booger (Coke). It looked like a fluffy marshmallow in a sandwich bag. After untying the knot, he dumped out a pile onto the marble countertop. He whipped out a black American Express card, and began slicing the coke. Dividing it into several lines for the crew. He dug in his pocket again. This time, pulling out a Fifty dollar bill from the balled up wad of cash. He rolled into a perfect straw circumference, and snorted the white line like Scarface in the 80's. The powder disappeared into the Fifty. "Whooo... Ahh....Shit" Sparkz mumbled, pinching his nostrils and sneezing. His pupils grew, and sweat rolled down his forehead. "Monty, you fuck around son?" He asked, offering me the straw shaped bill. "Of course I have, especially in Vegas and before shows sometimes." That's what I thought to myself. However, I didn't want my boss thinking I took part in drugs. So, I played the role like I never done it before, and like I was surprised that he even had it. Sparkz said "Loosen up, you with the Big Dogs tonight. Everything is on us! We got you. GET LIVE NIGGA!" I answered "Naw bro. I ain't never fucked around. But Fuck it though! I'm turnin up to the max tonight!"

I Snatched the bill from him, and stuck it in my right nostril. All eyes was on me. "Snniiffff!!" The burn rushed up my nose immediately. "Ohhhh Weee" I uttered, tasting the coke as it filtered from my nose and into my mouth. Everybody busted up laughing. "Don't hurt yourself now. You still got work on Monday!" A raspy voice said from the corner of the room. "Shut up nigga, I got this." I rebutted. Sparkz picked up where he left off. "That left nostril getting mad lonely. Show her some love my nigga." I stuffed the bill in my other nostril and carried out the order. "Snniiffff!" My head spun, then I started feeling a jolt of energy and excitement. "Got Damn!" I handed the bill to Josh with clammy palms. "Here, that's all you homie!" The room cheered me on, like I hit a game winning shot in the finals. "That's how you do it B! Ohh yeah, this nigga go wild out tonight!" I began to loosen up. These cats are cool. Well, it was finally time for action. Sparkz said

"C'mon it's time to roll my niggaz." He opened a drawer and tossed me a set of car keys. "Ay Monty, Catch. You pushing the Benz tonight! She parked in the garage." He tossed me the keys. "Aww, hell yeah!" I said, My face lit up. "Aww hell yeah nothing. Don't crash my shit!" "Man, ain't nobody go crash yo shit. Just cuz I'm on the ankle express, dont mean I don't know how to whip." "Yeah aight" He said, skeptical of my driving skills. Sparkz told Josh to grab a handful of weed out of the turkey bag that was laying on the dining room table, next to the Tec-9. "Yo, bring her too. In case shit goes left, Remember what happened last time son" Josh grabbed the Tec. I wonder what happened last time. I didn't bother to ask.

We hopped on the elevator and rode it to the lower level garage. When we got off. He pointed to a pearl white Mercedes Benz AMG that was backed in one of the parking spaces. "There she go." I smashed the button on the key fob and hopped in. The leather, woodgrane, tv screens and soft blue led lights had a luxurious feel to it. I pushed the start button like I was playing a video game and listened to the engine purr. Sparkz and Jersey jumped in a crystal blue Supercharged Jaguar XF, and Josh opened the door of a Racing Green Tesla Roadster. His other two business partners piled into a Black Cadillac Escalade. The sounds of engines roaring and idling echoed throughout the garage. One by one, we slowly pulled out into the city lights. Sparkz tapped the horn and stuck his head out the moon roof. "Yo..We're gonna follow Josh. This nigga knows how to get there on the backstreets."

Once we made it to the dark lonely roads, on cue they all took off. "Vroooom " We begin flying down the backstreets like it's the motorway speedway. I dont even wanna drive this niggaz car this fast. But fuck it. Gotta keep up with the pack. I stepped on the gas until it was on the floor. The dash told me she was running 90 mph. One by one we drifted around corners and flew past big trees. Occasionally swerving through oncoming traffic to cut in front of each other and race. We were seeing what these cars are made of. "Ohhhh shhiitt!" Skii Rrrttt! Tires began screeching, and brake lights lit up the night sky. I was inches away from rear ending Sparkz Jaguar! A family of deer was crossing the street. Josh barely missed them. "Whoooo, that was a close one!" I thought to myself. I would hate to crash this muthafucka. I'll be working for this nigga till im eighty to pay this car off, with the money im making. After the deer galloped across the street. Engines revved and we put the pedal to the metal like nothing ever happened.

After thirty minutes of racing and passing Starlight Drive-In Theatre. We finally arrived at the spot. The big white sign hanging from the building read "Club Blaze" in bright red lights. We pulled up in the parking lot looking like rap stars in a music video. Everybody marveled at the motorcade of luxury cars, that tiptoed by with music blasting. The parking lot was crowded. We hopped out and tossed the keys to the valet. Sparkz cashed him out for the whole crew. "Keep the change." We walked in the door and held our arms out. "Hey Hey, welcome to Blaze." The big black security guards scanned our id's and patted us down for weapons. We were clear. "Aight now, yaw boys have a good time." We belled in and huddled up under the colorful strobe lights that were flashing. I peeped the scene. My eyeballs almost fell out of their sockets. I was surrounded by big titties and bubble butts. Naked women of all different skin tones and body types, was twerking and performing acrobatics on the pole. Or, they was walking around flirting before offering a lap dance (for a fee of course). The bass from the speakers vibrated through the club. Boom, Boom. " We got- Racks on Racks on Racks" YC and Future had the club lit. Sparkz turned into a live wire. "Ay, let's get a section and some bottles!"

He flagged down a waitress that was passing by, and began whispering in her ear. She escorted us to a private section behind the velvet rope. We sat on the couches. "Yo.. Monty what you drinking?" He answered his own question. "Matta of fact I know what he want. Hey bartender..get this nigga a Old English" The section bursted out in laughter. Ha ha ha ha. He tapped my shoulder. "Im just fucking with you kid. What you drinking though?" Smirking I said "Fuck you man. Uhm, I'll do a shot of patron and a heineken." He looked at me like he was disappointed. "A shot? A Heneiken? Oh my God...What!?" The crew shook their heads. Boastfully he said "Let me get two bottles of patron! A bucket of heinys. Yo, what's the name of Jays shit? Oh yeah, and let me do three bottles of the Ace of Spades." "Alrighty, I got yaw." Said the bartender before walking off.

A few minutes later, bottle girls strutted toward us holding the bottles in the air with sparklers flickering. Everybody cleared the way, and watched to see who the bottles belonged to. We stood up in unison, grooving to the beat. The D.J. Shorted us out "I see yaw boys!" Jersey stood up on the couch and said "Lets ball niggaz!" Josh began to fill the cups up. We toasted and tossed back two shots. A medley of naked women came into our section. Every skin tone and body type made

Debt, Guns, and Dope

they way over. All eyes were on us! Sparkz discretely reached into his pocket pulled out a wad of cash and handed it to me. Jersey and his two business partners followed suit. Before I could thank them, they cut me off. "Just have some fun!" I flagged down the stallion that was standing across from me. She walked over to me and sat on my lap. "Damn, baby you gorgeous! What's your name?" She blushed. "Thank you. Fantasy. You cute! Wats yo name?" "Monty" "Ok then, Monty where u from?" "Cali" "Uh oh! West Coast in da buildin." She started giving me a lap dance. I grabbed a bottle of Ace and started chugging. Then I reached in my pocket started throwing money in the air. Sparkz and the crew were cheering me on like proud fathers. "There you go! Now that's how you turn up my nigga." He pulled out the bag of coke and handed it to the stripper that was bouncing on his lap. She stuck her pinky nail in the bag and scooped. After taking a few bumps, she scooped again and set the pinky nail under sparks nose. He sniffed and handed the bag to me. I dug the benz key in the bag and scooped out a serving. Sniifff! Sniff! "Oh My God!" The lights got brighter and the music got clearer. I'm in super party mode now. I started throwing more money in the air. I was making it rain on them hoes. I started feeling like I was a rich nigga, like this was my life. Although it wasn't, It was for the night and I was loving every second of it. I was getting a taste of how it felt to be rich. To ball hard. There was no looking back now. After motorboating some titties and taking a few more shots and lines. Josh tapped me on the shoulder. "L.Boogie, let me holla at you fam."

He wanted to speak in private. I got up and walked alongside him. "Everything straight bro?" I asked. "Oh yeah. Everything is Gucci. You havin a good time man?" Slurring my words and smiling cheek to cheek, I burped and said "IM haVing the TIme of MY LIFE bRo! Shit.. I'm on one!..These hOES in here looking Magically Delicious! What's up my nigga?" He said" C'mon let's go shoot some pool. Relax bruh. These broads ain't goin nowhere." We hit the pool table and racked 'em up (Prepared table for new game). Josh said "Yo.. On some real shit, don't think we brought you here just because you hit budget a few times and got promoted to manager." I was all ears. "Naw, not at all family! Understand something. We've had plenty of people get a promotion, and we didn't bring them into the fold like this." I called, purple side pocket. He continued "You're here because you have a lot of potential and we like your hustle. Don't think we didn't run your file (Ask around to check my authenticity). You a stand up nigga bruh!" "Appreciate that, Good lookin." We bumped fist. Josh continued "Just stay down and keep doin what you doin. You're going to elevate. Word up. We might have some other opportunities for you too. We got our hands in a few different ventures outside of collections. Orange corner pocket!" "Im wit it homie! Just keep me posted. Shit..I'm hungrier than a hostage on the third day."

Mid shot, Sparkz and the crew walked up and gathered around the pool table. "I got winner. Burp..I am DRUNK AS FUCK right now!" He put his arm around my shoulder. "But YO...I got an announcement to make!" Everybody leaned in. "I wanna tell you.. The reason we brought you out tonight, is to let you know WE WANNA BRING YOU ON THE TEAM! And let you know that you OFFICIALLY PART OF THE CREW! We also are going to bless you with ya own shop (Collection Agency). CONGRATULATIONS son!" They bombarded me with claps, cheers and handshakes. I was so happy and surprised that it felt surreal. Our business partner poured up a round of shots and we threw them back. "Whoooo!" He said "Yo, we're gonna go check out some office spaces next week. Find you a shop that seats like ten - fifteen collectors. Man, we go get this money!" I was locked in. They made me feel like a part of the family with every handshake. Suddenly, Sparkz wiped the smile off his face and got serious. With a cold stare he looked me dead in my eyes. The squad followed suit. "Now that you are down with the team, you family. Anybody fuck with you, they fuck with all of us! Word to mutha. And we expect the same out of you!" I nodded my head in agreement. I'm from the streets. I knew exactly what that meant. He continued. "Another thing, what happens in Vegas stays in Vegas, ya heard." (No snitching) Beady eyes and menacing stares grilled me from across the pool table, as Sparkz gave me the commandments of the crew. "Dont cross nobody on the team, cus niggaz will have to…(He wanted to say kill me, but realized he was in public) You know what I mean! We fucks wit you, and we wanna see you come up Monty. You cut from the same pedigree as us. Now, enough about business. LETS HAVE SOME FUCKIN FUN MY NIGGAZ!!" The cold stares transformed back into smiles and proud facial expressions. Josh rolled up a blunt, we poured up another round of shots and proceeded to play pool. "Eight ball, top pocket." Bang!

After hours of taking shots, getting lap dances and snorting lines. Jersey uttered "Yo, my stomach is touchin my back right now. I'm hungry as shit." Sparkz said "I feel you! Niggaz do need to put sumthin on they stomachs. Ayyy.. Whoooo!" He was flagging down a big tittied waitress. "Hey baby, what ya need?" Slurring his speech he said "Let me do like a hunnid wings, wit sum fries." "How u want em dun?" "Uhh.. Lemon Peppa, do some Extra Hot. And uhm.. Let me get some mild with the lemon peppa sprinkles. And can you bring us some bottled woddahs too. Thank you sexy!" She repeated the order. Sparkz leaned over and said "Yo Monty. Just drive ya self home. I'll get the whip from you tomorrow. I'll probably have you drive to my crib and I'll take you back home or somethin. I don't know, we'll figure it out. No biggie. You need to be trying to bag one of these bitches in here" "I'm already ten steps ahead of you Bro. You see her over there. She been choosy Suzy all night. I already knocked her. (Got the phone number)""Oh yeah?" "Yup, baby go slide through (come over) when she gets off." We slapped hands "Okay I see you!"

Cost to start an office:

1. 7 cpu (complete system) @ $150.00 per =$1,050.00 and 3 Apple Mac Cpu @ $6,200.00

2. 10 desk(or cubicles) @ $100.00 per =$1,000.00

3. Phone System Thru Vonage 10 lines @ $500.00 or $125 a month for 3 extensions (Fast Pbx pho service)

4. Hard Phones 10 phones@$125.00=$1,250.00

5. Data Base Thru Simplicity Collection @ $750.00 or $200 Per User (with no monthly fees through Collection Max)

6. Debt Portfolio @ $20,000 Face value of portfolio $2m and $10,000 for Premium Portfolio

7. Four Cubicles with drawers @ $7,383.00 (www.bizchair.com)

8. Security Cameras $1,500.00 (www.brandsmartusa.com)

9. H.P. Office Paper $55.00 a Case (4 cases a week) $1,120 a month @ Staples

10. H.P. Color Laser Printer, Fax, Copier $579.00 (www.store.hp.com)

11. Two Office desk (Owner/ Manager) $1,918.00

12. Pens, Calculators, Sticky Notes Ect... $200.00

13. Office Space $900.00 -$1,500.00 a month

14. Payroll = Two Operations Managers $4,800 a month

   Payroll = One Admin $2,080 a month

   Payroll = Four Collectors/ Employees $7,680 ($12 an hour, 40 hours a week)

15. Petty Cash or Cash Prize Give Outs $5,000 ($2,500cash and $2,500credit card)

16. Ten Office Chairs @ $3,500 (7cpu chairs, 3exec chairs)

******1 time Cost to get Started $ 51,576 *****

Month to Month Cost with 4 month Reserved

1. 10 collectors @ $10.00 hours w/160 hours per month=$64K for 4 months

2. Phone system @ $500.00 per month=$2,000

3. Tlo skip tracing tool @150.00 per month=$600.00

4. Rent for the Office Space = $3,600 - $6,000

Total Cost For 4 month Reserve = $72,600

I boogied from Blaze, and made it home DUI and accident free (Thank God). Just as planned, Fantasy pulled up around 4am. We spent over an hour having Wild, Rough, Erotic sex. She was flexible and freaky! I blacked out shortly after. "Hey..Monty, Monty. Come lock the door. I'm bout to leave." She was shaking me. "Ok. Ok. I'm up! What time is it?" My head was spinning. "Almost ten." I walked her to the door. After a kiss on the cheek, I went right back to sleep. A few hours later Sparkz tapped my line.

"Monty! Rise and shine. Rise and Grind." Still groggy I said "Top of the morning." "How was ya night last night? You didn't crash my shit did you?" "Naw.. I don't plan on workin for you forever my nigga." "Ha, Ha.No Doubt." "But anyways, I told you I was gonna G.T.D." "G.T.D.?" He sounded puzzled. "Got The Drawers Dogg!" I said, sounding like Tommy from Martin. Sparkz laughter echoed through the phone. "Yo.. You a funny nigga. Pull up to my crib son. We'll go get some Waffle House, then I'll shoot you to the crib." "Aight, I'm bout to pull up." I jumped on 75 North to Buckhead and landed at Sparkz penthouse. He was briefing me on how his night ended " I ended up fuckin that thick ass Puerto Rican bitch, that kept coming in our section. I was goin crazy in her shit yo. She was screaming mad loud..I, Papi, Papi, Papi!" Smiling and giving him his props I said "I feel you homie. Shit, last night I put so much dick in her, she thought she was a pair of boxers" Sparks laughed uncontrollably. "You a ill nigga L.Boogie! That's why I fuck wit you." "Likewise " We hopped in the Benz and he took me back to the gates. On the way home I told myself, I'm glad that I came out. I almost blew a golden opportunity. We pulled in front of my building. Before getting out of the car, Sparkz gave me a stern reminder "Don't forget. What happens in Vegas stays in Vegas!" "'Say Less."

4.

CH:7 Steppin on da Product

Mac Davenport

CHAPTER 7
STEPPIN ON THE PRODUCT

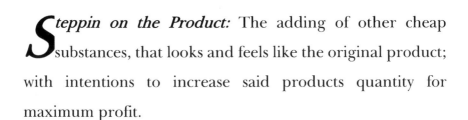

*S**teppin on the Product:* The adding of other cheap substances, that looks and feels like the original product; with intentions to increase said products quantity for maximum profit.

In the dope game, the dealer and or plug who wants to maximize their profits will step on the product. For example, you have the cocaine dealer who cuts his coke with baby Similac to turn one ounce to two. Or, like the main stream Parmesan Cheese companies who cut their work with wood pulp or sawdust. Don't forget the cunning weed dealer who sells a pound of weed, with a few ounces of it being Peat moss from your local Home Depot's garden department. In the streets of Debt Collections, you got dealers (Debt Brokers) steppin on the Product too.

Cooking up accounts. In other words, they alter/ edit the debt portfolio (which comes on an excel spreadsheet) by changing the date that the debtor took out the loan. Also, by changing the charge off dates (the date the loan went into default). That way, the accounts don't appear to be past the statute of limitations. Which is seven Years, and before its deemed uncollectible and must be removed from the credit report with all three bureaus. Doing this makes the accounts appear to be newer than they truly are. As a result making them more valuable. That same portfolio could also be sold to multiple agency owners. All they gotta do is add the new owners name along with his companies name, on the Chain of Title to the Debt. That makes them feel real comfortable. The Chain of title to the debt is the proof of ownership. Similar to receiving the title for a car that you purchased. But be careful! Finessing the wrong person can be deadly.

I looked at my phone, it was 7:43 a.m. Fuck I'm bout to miss the bus. I grabbed my backpack and bolted out the door. I sprinted pass some niggas sharing a Newport at the bus stop. "Ay! Did the 186 come already?" Hell naw, not yet. they said in unison. Cool, I thought to myself. I got time to tap this blunt a few times before the bus pulled up. Shortly after smashing the end of the blunt against the concrete, the bus pulled up Flashing 186 to Mcafee Rd. I let people cut in front of me, while I doused myself in cologne trying my best to hide the Skunky weed smell relaxing on my shirt and fingertips. Once on the bus I closed my eyes trying to get a cat nap. I was still tired plus my head was pounding. I got off at Five Points train station and waited for the train that took me to my job. Every day it took me about two hours to get to work. I arrived at work around 11 something. The problem is my shift started at 10:00a.m.

"What's Wrong Davenport? They don't teach yaw how to read clocks in California?" Said My manager in a sarcastic southern accent!

"Damn Tish, you know I'm taking a two-hour pilgrimage on the bus to get here! Cut a brotha some slack. Y'all need to start giving out company cars! And I wouldn't have these problems."

She laughed and said "Boooyyy Bye.!! Yo ass knew how far this damn job was when you filled out that application." Walking to my cubicle, I scoffed True, True. After setting down my backpack, I headed straight for the coffee pot. I filled my cup to the brim. No cream, no sugar; and slithered back to my seat while Tish had her back turned having sidebar conversation about Love and Hip Hop episodes. It always pisses off managers when you come in late and don't get straight to work. I Put my headset on and started calling my declines (Debtors who bounced payments). Ring, Ring, Ring....

Debtor: This is Kathy

Me: Hey, this is Mr. Davenport here with Kaufman, Morris and associates. Please be advised This call is being monitored and or recorded for quality assurance and training, Ok.

Debtor: Ok, but can I ask you what this is about?

Me: Well, the nature of the call is… We have a returned bank item for $1,256.34. I was hoping…

Before I could finish my sentence, I heard screaming from the front of the office like somebody was being stabbed to death. It came from where the receptionist sits. It was followed up by two men's voices.

Goon 1: "Shut the Fuck Up Bitch". A goon mushed her face with a pistol. Call your Punk ass Boss and put 'em on speaker. The other gunmen walked down the aisle of the cubicles.

"Everybody hang the muthafuckin phone up."

This one collector either thought shit was a joke, didn't hear them say get off the phone or he was really trying to get a payment. Whatever the case was, he made a terrible mistake. He was leaning in his cubicle talking low.

"Okay ma'am, help me to help you. If you can do at least $750, I can speak with my supervisor and possibly…."

The armed gunmen walked toward the agent and stood behind him calmly, like he was a manager about to assist him with the call. Gritting his teeth, with a raspy voice, he said "Nigga, you didn't hear what the fuck I said" and with all the power in his arm, he swung the chrome plated pistol like a boxer throwing a hook and hit the dude square in his mouth. The impact from the blow knocked the headset off his head. Dude started crying and screaming, while trying to hold up the now dangling, broken jaw. Blood, tears, and pieces of his chipped teeth rushed to the floor headfirst causing an instant stain on the tan carpet.

"Now when we tell yaw Fuck boys and Ugly bitches to do somethin. Yaw do it, I ain't playin!" the southern accent said in a serious tone, while waving the blood-stained pistol at all the collectors in the office. He closed out his treacherous Talk Off strong. "Now, one of yaw better get yo lame ass boss on the phone, or I swear befo God... ima kill one of yaw shawty. We not playin behind our money!"

Shaking and crying, one of the team leads handed the goon her android. She softly mumbled "He wants to talk to you" Snatching the phone out her hand and shooing her away, he yelled in to the phone "What's up Bruh, now you wanna take a niggaz call" he walked into the managers office, and closed the door behind him. I guess he needed some privacy while he was making terroristic threats. While he was on the phone with our boss, the other two gunmen kept a watchful eye on us. These niggas was eating donuts from out the break room and doing they best to keep us calm and quiet while the ring leader deliberated. About 5 minutes passed by before the door swung open, and the goon hastily walked out of the office slightly calmer. The raspy voice said to his crew "C'mon, we outta here, Bruh said he'll meet us in the park and lot at the Lenox Mall." They stormed out, as the last goon walked backwards toward the door pointing the gun at us until he was out of the out of sight.

Management immediately called 911! The police showed up to interview the few collectors who stuck around until they arrived. Mostly everybody left, as I can guarantee we were getting sent home early anyway, after an incident like that. We were called individually and told that we are being temporarily furloughed and the office will be closed until further notice. H.R. reinsured us that we will be paid as normal, and we would receive a call and or email giving us a date to report back to work. That never happened though. After getting recruited to Sparkz crew, getting my own shop, buying and selling debt and hanging out with the big fish in the game. I found out why those goons ran up in my former bosses trap like that. It turns out he was stepping on the product (debt) while getting loans from dope boys. Selling them dreams of cleaning up their money by investing in debt portfolios, computers and offices. Having dope boys help with payroll and all kinds of shit. Also, using their money to buy coke, cars and clothes. Another cardinal sin. See, he was supposed to remit a check to them every month. You know, cut them in on the profits. Especially with them being silent investors/ business partners. He was extra disrespectful and out of line. Spending their money, while screening their calls and rarely showing up at the office to be confronted. Leaving his managers to run the operation and screen visitors. He had it coming. Word is, he was over 50k in debt. I'm surprised they didn't kill him. They was about to. That clown wasn't the only person stepping on the product. I soon learned it was a standard business practice. After about a year of running my own shop and proving my loyalty, work ethic and being trustworthy. I finally got let into the loop all the way. On a rainy Thursday evening after work, Josh told me "A Mont stick around. I need to talk to you." It sounded serious.

After all the collectors cleared out of the office and it was just me and him, he opened up a Macbook. He said. "Grab a seat, fam. And pay close attention. Im only gonna show you this shit once." I was all ears. "Better yet, grab a pen. Take notes!" This was like the owner of Coca-Cola bringing you into the vault and showing you the recipe. He said, "This is how we make the big bucks." Josh was giving me the game on how to step on the product or how to cook up accounts. He clicked on Excel and opened a spreadsheet containing a debt portfolio. The show began. He clicked on one of the columns that had the account balance. It read $388. Josh pointed at the screen "You see this balance right here?" He deleted the $388 and typed in $896.22. Laughing, He said. "That's fees and interest." Scrolling down the spreadsheet he did the same thing to about ten accounts."Alright you get the picture." I couldnt believe they were doing this to thousands and thousands of accounts. This would become one of my duties inside the organization. These niggaz were essentially, turning a debt portfolio with a $100,000 face value into a quarter of a million dollars. Simply by increasing the balance. He moved on to the column that read open date (when loan was issued) then to the charge off date (when loan went in default). He highlighted the column. "You see this charge off date?" "Yup" Josh smashed the backspace, deleting the 2008. He typed in 2010. He also proceeded to change all the bankruptcy accounts to new status. The accounts that reflected PIF (paid in full), were converted to delinquent balances. Making it appear as though they never paid a buffalo nickel.

"This is how we get money around here, my nigga! Welcome to the team." Last but not least, he pulled up a template of the "Chain of Title to the Debt." The print on it looked like an award from a school. "You see this here?" He clicked on the field with the owner's name. He proceeded to delete it. He said "Whenever we sell a portfolio, we put the new owner's name here" He typed in John Doe to give me an example. He pressed the tab key and jumped to the next line. "You see where it says Company name." He deleted it and typed 1, 2, 3 services. "This is where we enter the name of the company. You feel me" I took notes. He continued "Every time we sell a debt portfolio, this is what we email them. We also give them a printed copy." He had me read the legal jargon, essentially stating they are now the owner of the debt and reserve the right to liquidate the portfolio. I was blown away after learning the ropes and watching him alter the files. Us collectors were professional scammers and didn't even know it. It all made sense why they trained collectors the way they did. We were taught, if a debtor claims they paid but didn't have a Paid in Full letter, to follow through and collect that debt. We were making people pay the bill twice for failure to keep up with their documentation.

It also filled in the gaps of my confusion. It answered, why so many people claimed they took the loan out years ago, and not on the date that I was alleging. I wrote it off as them having a short-term memory or them trying to wiggle their way out of paying the bill. I guess not. After giving me a tutorial on stepping on the product, and cooking up accounts, he closed the laptop. "Alright.. Let's roll, I'll take you to the crib. Don't tell nobody what you saw here!" "Say Less!"

CHAPTER 8: THE MERCHANT

Mad Davenport

CHAPTER 8
THE MERCHANT

Merchant Processor: Also known as a merchant bank, acquirer, or acquiring financial institution, is a financial institution that processes payment card transactions for merchants. They act as a mediator between banks, customers, and merchants.

-Google

In the dope game, nothing is more important than "The Money." What else would you be risking your life, safety and freedom for? From a low-level dealer up to a semi-successful dealer, you might not be at the level where you need assistance counting and managing your bread. A hood accountant might be a bad investment for you at this juncture. But, for the high profile dealers generating so much money they can't handle it alone, it's mandatory they hire a trustworthy buffer to help them count, launder, manage and sometimes invest their money. Well in the collections business, The Merchant plays that role. Hands down, the Merchant is the most valuable commodity to a collection agency outside of the debt portfolio and the collectors. Without a merchant processor, there is absolutely no way that a collection agency can make money. Collection agencies are deemed as high risk companies and it is extremely difficult to find a merchant that will process payments for them. If you are fortunate enough to find a merchant willing to gamble on your company. They normally charge a fee of 3% - 7% per payment processed. Or, they take the above percentages of your total earnings per month. Depending on your agency and the condition of your personal credit. Merchants Processing companies also require you to have a reserve of in the account. Anywhere from $2,500 up to $5,000. This cash reserve is their insurance policy, making sure they can always get their money back from a charged back payment. Sometimes debtors pay their bill and then call their back claiming they don't recognize the transaction.

I reminisce about being on break talking to my co-workers, while they pulled on a Newport or Black and Mild. They used to say "Yeah girl I'm telling you, I'm bout to buy some paper bitch (a debt portfolio) and start collecting for myself at da house." Flicking ashes and shaking hands "I'm just sayin, do da math! Like..if we already collecting $10,000 a month in here, that's $120,000 a year right there. I already kno where to get some good paper! Shit, I'll put you on too. Pay you 50% commission. Bitch think about it, if we collectin for ourselves we really would go hard. Probably be doin like 20 thou a month." The conversation always dies when the boss or manager walks by. Their calculations are accurate. However, they fail to realize they lack the discipline to work from home, The L.L.C documentation, and the personal credit for a merchant to get it poppin.

I used to sound just like those girls. Thinking it was as easy as buying a portfolio, getting a 1-800 number and making $10,000 a month for myself. But I didn't realize, or no one ever told me that I needed a merchant processor. My first rodeo, me and the homie Alex, were working for this agency and ended up being cool with the owner's son. He was a collector too, and the first person I ever brought a portfolio from. I'll never forget. We were so excited that day. He told us he would hook us up with some decent paper for pennies on the dollar. He said "The portfolio has five hundred accounts in it. Uhm, roughly $20,000 face value. It's a mixture of credit cards and payday loans. I'll give it to you guys for about 200 bucks." He knew we didn't have a merchant, but that didn't stop him from selling it to us though. Me and the homie put up a hundred a piece and cashed out the portfolio. One day after work, we met up with Rod at the Burger King in Dunwoody. We sat down, ate some burgers, and talked a little business. After giving him the cash he emailed us the files. He also gave us a few behind the scenes jewels on the collections business. You couldn't tell us we weren't bosses at that moment. We had a debt portfolio! We also didn't realize that you need some sort of collection software to upload the debt portfolio into. If not, all you have is a spreadsheet with phone numbers, names, emails, addresses, the name of the company they got the loan from, the balance owed and things of that nature. Now granted, you can call the numbers off of the spreadsheet and try to collect like that, but it is extremely difficult.

It is mandatory, or strongly suggested that you have some sort of collection software. We tried using a software called Collections Max. It was an old school software that offered a free version. The only drawback is you can't do a batch import. Meaning upload thousands of accounts with a few clicks of the mouse. You must upload each account into the system manually (one by one). Meaning type in the debtor's name, address, each phone number (Cell, job, references, ect.) Type in the place of employment, Lender, Social Security number, so on and so forth. Can you imagine having to do this for one thousand accounts? We did upload over one hundred accounts manually, and we attempted to call and collect directly off of the spreadsheet. It was a headache though. Especially trying to notate and keep track of accounts worked. In saying all that, we too found out that you need a merchant to run a collection agency. If we were to get a payment and get the credit card number from these people, how the hell would we get the money off their credit card? and into our pockets. We had a real dilemma.

As mentioned, collection agencies are what they call high risk companies. So therefore, merchants rarely want to handle their processing needs. Mainly because of the high volume of chargebacks. And also because of the deceptive practices that collection agency owners use to collect the debt. Merchants do not want to be associated with that type of business. They're usually reserved for sales, retail and things of that nature. POS (point of sale systems) are their bread and butter too.

When you go to a gas station or a market, and you swipe or tap your debit card, you're normally using a POS system.

When those funds come off of your card, the merchant will hold them in their reserve or their bank account. Once those funds clear your bank, meaning you didn't charge it back. In other words, call your bank and say you don't recognize the transaction and it is fraud. As long as those funds clear on your end, they will be delegated to the company. Well, I wish I would've known all this shit before I purchased the portfolio. But it takes money to make money and it's never a loss. It's a lesson. Alex and I ended up finding a lady who, I won't say her name, had a collection agency. She allowed us to process payments through her merchant at a 20% rate, meaning she will keep 20% of every payment that she processed for us. If we got a $100 payment, $20 belonged to her.

Well, in all that being said, that didn't last long at all. We were still working nine to five jobs and also we weren't able to work the account the way that an account needs to properly be worked. Meaning, when we are at work collecting for someone else between nine to five, those are the hours that we need to be contacting our debtors. By the time we got off work and tried to call a few accounts, if they did return our call during the day, we will be at work. So it just never panned out. We didn't have the time or energy and besides, we also didn't have any skip tracing software and the accounts were never scrubbed. So the only phone numbers that were on file were the old ones used from the original loan application. People move and change numbers though over the years. We had numbers for the references that were used when the loan and or credit card was initially taken out. With the credit card or loan being four to five years old or delinquent, it's a nine times out of ten chance that those numbers are no good. They are now disconnected and the debtor has a new number. That's why it's imperative that those accounts are skip traced.

These days, I am able to get updated phone numbers on the debtor. The most recent number to their cell, place of employment, as well as friends, family members and associates. Thankfully, with me having my own shop and having Sparkz as a business partner, I am able to process payments though my own merchant.

I can also recall desperate measures of trying to get payments processed. If getting a debtor on the phone, we would tell them, send a MoneyGram and we will send you a confirmation code letting you know that your payment has been processed. The only problem with that is with all the Craigslist scams and all the Nigerian scams, people were very, very skeptical of sending moneygrams and western unions.

When you have a merchant processor, they are able to see the name of the entity that ran that payment. Also, having a merchant processor gives you credibility as a collector when you're telling someone "Okay ma'am you will see Highland Financial Services, our merchant processor, on your bank statement letting you know that we're the ones who ran your payment. Also, having the merchants 1-800 number on their bank statement to contact. Helping to validate your company. But when you're having someone go send a money gram or western union to your company, it just seems like a scam.

When you're in the trenches though, desperate times calls for desperate measures. Me and A. Boogie didn't give up though, we also used Square. With Square, they only allowed payment processing for retail or small time boutiques or online sales. But see, we had to alter that application. Ya dig! But after getting a high volume of payments for $1,400 here, $500 here, $200 here, $50 here, they immediately froze up all of our funds. We had a $1,700 payment that was scheduled to be dropped the next day. I was counting that money and spending it before I even got it. We had received an email from Square saying that it was a fraudulent transaction and that they would have to conduct an investigation. Once the investigation is complete, the funds will be released within seven to fourteen business days. As long as everything checked out. Well, we never did get that money. They also locked those funds and closed down our square merchant account. That put the nail in the coffin of our business.

Getting a merchant processor requires them doing a personal credit check, verifying your business account, andand bank statements. Verifying your business license and L.L.C documentation and all. A handful of collectors have bad credit when they're sitting in that cubicle. They have the skills to generate 100k a year. However, It's not as easy as it seems to get a merchant and start collecting on your own debt.

That's one of the advantages that collection agency owners have over the collector. They normally have good personal credit, a business license and the capital to obtain a merchant processor account. The average collector working a nine to five job doesn't have $5,000 just sitting around like that. Along with the cheese to buy a debt portfolio and still pay their rent while waiting on the business to grow.

This is the main component, the merchant, the most important asset to a collection agency. No merchant equals no money. This is the main barrier between collection agency owners and collectors. Anybody can get their hand on a debt portfolio, but everybody is not capable of getting a merchant processor account to get that money off of the debtor's debit card and in to your back account!

When I first got my keys to the trap, and started rising to the top of the collection game, one of the first rules I was told about the merchant is: "Never live out of the merchant account!" That means not spending the money as soon as it hits the business checking account. Doing so, is the equivalent to the drug dealer spending his re-up money (the money needed to buy more drugs). As I stated, when a payment gets processed and those funds are drafted from the debtor's debit card. Within one to three business days, you will get that deposit into your business checking account. And when your company is doing numbers, like $10,000 - $30,000 a day or more, seeing that kind of money and those big deposits hitting that business account can be tempting to spend, to the undisciplined hustler. Before they know it, they find themselves spending it, partying with it, and making unnecessary purchases. Even though you're racking in that money, Don't forget, you still have to pay rent.

You also have to make payroll. Your collectors are the backbone of the organization and it's mandatory they get paid in full on time. You have to pay the expenses of the trap.

You have to pay for coffee. You have to pay for the debt software. You have to be able to buy more debt or more work. You also have to be able to pay for the lights, the internet, the monthly phone bill for your 1-800-NUMBERS and things of that nature. The last thing you want to do is start living out of that merchant account and can't afford to make the necessary payments to keep the operation going. It's been too many times where I've seen agency owners come to their employees and say: "Hey, your checks are a little bit short. I can get the rest to you on Friday or in a day or two. I'm waiting for some payments to clear!" Or, the owner who catches the collector by surprise. Handing them a check knowing the bank won't cash it because there's no money in the business account. The collector is none the wiser, until the bank teller slides them back the signed check and softly says: "You may want to contact your company, there isn't enough funds in the business account for me to cash this check, I'm sorry honey."

"I have to get you back next Friday." That's the worst thing you can do and say, as you'll suck the life force right out of your collectors. They will no longer be ambitious or eager to come to work and collect for you. They feel played, like they worked two weeks for nothing. Also, it puts a bad stain on you as an agency owner or as a plug, because it shows that you got your soldiers and your workers out there trapping, but you can't afford to pay them. It's always a bad look. You never want to live out of the merchant. Living a lifestyle that you can't afford. You would rather pay your employees and make sure that they eat before you receive a check if need be.

I learned another top rule when dealing with the merchant. You NEVER want to have a high chargeback rate by any means. That is the number one factor that can get your merchant closed down and funds frozen. With that being said, your collectors are your frontline soldiers. They're responsible for setting up good payment arrangements and not pissing off the debtor. Doing everything in their power to paint the picture that the company is legitimate and not a scam. The minute that a debtor gets the inkling that this may be a scam, is the moment that they will call their bank and say that "This is fraud, I don't recognize this transaction from ABC services" and the money will go back to the debtor. Repossessing that payment from you and your company. Too many chargebacks, is one of the main factors that results in merchant processors closing down your merchant account and locking up all of your funds sitting in that reserve. That is the last thing that you want to happen. This would be the equivalent of the kingpin not having access to his money in his safe house. It's business suicide, because you lose your money earned and ability to make money moving forward. Your collectors can't get paid, you can't pay your bills, and shit starts going downhill from there. All the payments that you and your collectors have scheduled to run cannot get processed. Take heed!

Chapter 9: Burn da Client (run off on da plug)

Mad Davenport

CHAPTER 9
BURN THE CLIENT (RUN OFF ON DA PLUG)

In the dope game, sometimes dealers run off on the plug. Meaning, they will keep his product and money without paying him for it. They ignore his calls and go awol, when it's time to pay up. One of the many pet peeves of the plug. Giving out a package, only to never see any of the proceeds. Believe it or not the same thing happens in collections all the time. Debt brokers and or agency owners looking to franchise and expand their operation, invest in new up and coming owners. Sometimes get burnt by doing this. They will lease office space, provide the debt, computers, and merchant processor. They also leave you with the responsibility of hiring collectors and running the operation. This is normally done on a 60% - 40% contingency split. Meaning the investor is compensated 60% of every payment processed and the owner is left with 40%. These numbers can fluctuate and be negotiated, depending on how much capital the new owner is bringing to the table, and if he already has debt. In collections when a slippery owner runs off on the plug, he closes down the office abruptly. Keeping the computers and all the payments that his collectors liquidated from the debt portfolio you provided. All monies collected go directly to his business account, as he probably already had his own merchant. You never see a dime when he disappears and stops taking your calls.

Setting somebody up with their own shop is like the collection agency. It's the equivalent of the kingpin setting up a new hustler or dealer up with their own drug operation. There's a few different ways that you can do this as a collection agency owner or a debt broker. When you're setting someone up with their own shop, that means helping them get their office space. Paying the deposit to ascertain the keys to the building, getting the cubicles for them, buying the computers, and providing the debt portfolio. Ohh yeah, and putting up the money for payroll to get the Collectors.

Normally the plug starts off investing ninety days worth of payroll. This standard time frame should give the up and coming owner enough time to stack their bread to cover payroll on their own. The generous plug with deep pockets, will sometimes invest six months worth of payroll upfront. If you're going into business with someone who has the money to get their own computers, cover their own payroll expenses, cubicles, office decor, ect. Then as the plug or debt broker, you can just provide the debt portfolio (work) the same way a plug provides a dealer the drugs to sell.

One night after work hours, me and the crew was taking shots of Patron in the conference room. Sparkz told a tale of him fronting a cat from Florida, a portfolio with a $200,000,000 face value. He was remitting payments every month like he was supposed to for over a year before going off the grid. Sparkz face lit up as he reminisced telling the story. "Ha Ha Ha..Yo, he was crying like a little bitch when I put the strap in his mouth. Please don't shoot me!, please don't shoot me!.. Ha Ha. Stoopid ass must have forgot about skip tracing. I found him at his moms lacking (caught off guard/not paying attention). I almost killed him! But I got respect for my elders. Word up! I just shot em in the stomach. I wasn't tryin to blow his brains out in front of his moms." Said Sparkz sarcastically. "Aww, Shut up! You wasn't go do shit! you getting rusty nigga." Josh interrupted. Laughter echoed through the conference room. The scandalous business owner had to find out the harsh consequences of running off on Sparkz. After months of goons staking out his office and the homes of family and friends, he paid that money back.

In the game of collections. People are always running off on the plug in different ways, shapes and forms. There's situations where the plug or debt broker will front millions of dollars worth of debt to an agency owner because they have plenty of debt but don't have collectors or people to trap for them. A fast talking agency owner will accept the debt portfolio (work) gladly. They don't have anything to lose and everything to profit, as they aren't spending any money upfront. They'll tell the plug "Yeah, I'll run your debt through my dialer system and see what it does. I have a team of Top Gun collectors. Email me the file, and I'll give you a check every month. You don't have to do anything but sit back and cash checks." It sounds good, right? All I have to do is give him a flash drive with the files on it, or email this debt portfolio and I can just go on about my life and get a check every month for thousands of dollars. Hey, who doesn't want to do that? But what you don't know is that owner is processing the collected payments through his merchant. Every day or every three days, deposits are going in, guess who's business checking account. Yup, you guessed it. Deposits in the amounts of, sometimes $2,000, sometimes $23,000. Maybe $500 or $40,000. If you have 10 collectors collecting $10,000 to $12,000 a month, that's easily generating $120,000 a month. Not to mention, money that's coming in from older payments or what we call post dates (payments that's automatically scheduled to be processed- previously collected payments.) What happens is the cunning agency owner makes hundreds of thousands without giving the plug a single penny. The game goofy plug or debt broker will typically call the owner and say, "Hey, what's going on? I haven't received a check yet! Is the paper (debt) any good? You haven't remitted any money." At that juncture, you have officially been burnt. Now the Top Gun closer comes out of the owner, as they Talk You off. Making you think that your debt is no good and their collectors weren't able to squeeze blood out of a turnip.

"Man, this portfolio is BullShit! You sold me some garbage paper! I got my collectors hammering the phones hard. Ain't no money in this debt. I've been running your files on the dialer five hours a day and cold calling. I scrubbed it (skip traced- find updated contact information) and everything!" They will say convincingly. "And on top of that, it's almost past the statute of limitation. Man, these people don't want to pay this shit! I still got to pay my collectors and the T.L.O bill (Skiptracing software). You should be cutting me a check for wasting my time." The game goofy owner doesn't know that he's being finessed. Chances are they're knocking it out the park, and making thousands. But he doesn't know because he doesn't have the books handy. And even if he does have access to them, those are subject to be cooked and altered at any moment. He's happy to receive any money at that point. The now disappointed plug may end the conversation along the lines of, "Well, just keep me posted. I could have sworn it was some pretty good debt. Just give me what you can, I have a family. Anything you can do!" After generating hundreds of thousands of dollars, possibly millions and milking that portfolio dry (bleeding it), for every penny they can liquidate.

That plug will never hear from them again. They will slowly break communication, if not just completely abandoning communication. Being that they have an office/trap and the plug knows the location, He will randomly pop up at the office occasionally. However, they will use their manager as a buffer to slowly brush him off. If they finally catch up to the slippery owner, he flips the script "You know what? Take the portfolio back. I'm going to pull it out of my dialer. We're not going to collect on it no more. We're losing money at this point." Feeling accomplished because they got their portfolio back. They leave, not realizing there accounts have been beat up. Each debtor has been called multiple times by different Top Gun closers, doing second talk offs and collecting the payments, or for the ones that's a refusal to pay, putting different voices on the call, in an attempt to turn that account around and turn 'em into a payer. He has been finessed. They worked his portfolio, bled every penny out of it and returned it back to you with no money. Handed you a fruit with no juice in it.

Once you go back to your existence and figure that you are just severing ties with that agency owner. You might say "Hey, I'm going to take this portfolio and sell it to somebody." Or, "You know what? I'm going to just get my own group of collectors and start collecting on this debt." But little do you know, the minute that you upload that debt into your software, the minute that you upload that debt into your automated dialing system and start pumping out calls, everybody that you get on the phone is going to give you some news that you cannot use. "I paid this already!" "This is settled." "I set up a payment arrangement on this already." "I'm already paying $200 a month to so-and-So agency." "I already did a thousand dollar settlement with so-and-So agency last month" "I gave $5,000 to So-and-So agency just yesterday" At that moment you realized that you've been jugged, you've been finessed. But by that time it's too late.

Cooking the books, is a way to pacify a plug before burning them. Emailing detailed reports, to substantiate the low numbers and justify why the plug is receiving little to know monthly checks for the debt they provided (work they fronted.) In so many words, if they have 10 collectors collecting $10,000 a month. That means that trap is generating $100,000 a month. If that owner is processing payments through their own merchant. By the time you get the books, it may say they only processed $72,000 that month. What you don't understand is the other 28,000 went directly into their checking account on top of the 40% that they were getting from you. As time goes on, they're slowly taking crumbs off the loaf and taking crumbs off of each piece of bread until they got their own loaf.

This same play is ran in the dope game by the sneaky dealer. Every time you give them a brick, they're pinching a few grams here and there. Then they turn around and tell the plug that someone else came up short. Even though they were pocketing money or pocketing extra work. Well, you also have the other type of crook, a greasy muthafucka that runs off on the plug straight up. No stealing little by little over time. Well, Tina and Kevin, they were those type of crooks. They just flat out ran, and Sparkz never seen it coming. See, they had the whole ambiance of being a square thing down to a science. They presented themselves as standup honest people. Kevin always wore nice slacks and penny loafers and polo button downs (tucked in) and shit, or always wore some suit. And Tina, she dressed really conservative, nice sundresses, little flats or wedges, never dressing, salacious or dressing erotic, scantily clothed. They always spoke very professionally and you never heard them curse. They played really cheesy and they may have really been like that to a certain degree, but they had it down packed where you couldn't smell it on them that they would rob you. They were the ones that robbed you with a smile on their face in a suit. Not the mask, gun, and get on the fucking floor.

I remember being at Sparkz office one day doing some training with a new group of collectors. When he told me he was setting up Tina and Kevin up with an office. He said it was a shop that could hold about 15 collectors in Stone Mountain. He gave them the whole operation, and when I say the whole operation, he provided them with the computers, the debt, the cubicles, and also he agreed to pay payroll for about four months until the business or the operation started generating some money. It was pretty much plug and play, almost like getting a franchise of a

McDonald's. And all you have to do is just hire the Cooks, cashiers and have them cook the food and make that money and run the place. No different than the kingpin getting you a building, house or an apartment to sell the drugs out of. Also, giving you the drugs, the baggies, scales, paying the electricity bill, and making sure that you're able to feed your soldiers and provide them guns.

See Sparkz was a real block boy cut from the streets. But as to my belief with Tina and Kevin, he let his guard down. He violated one of the rules of the game, which is no one is exempt from being under scrutiny. You don't let your guard down with anyone. See, he was too trusting with them just because they were clean cut and probably even because Tina was white. He didn't apply the same watchful eye that he did with niggas. With black people, he applied more pressure and indirectly threatened them like they were drug dealers working under him in his operation. But with Tina and Kevin, I noticed he spoke a little more professionally and treated them just like business partners or someone down at the bank. Tina and Kevin remitted on time for about five months, meaning on time payments were never a problem for Sparkz. Everything was going smooth until Tuesday morning after Labor Day. As we all know, Labor Days in North America fall on a Monday. Everyone usually has the day off work. People usually enjoy their day off. Barbecuing, enjoying time with the family, eating, getting drunk, and partying.

Well, while Sparkz, me and the rest of the world were barbecuing and enjoying our day off. Tina and Kev, they were busy. Hard at work, Robbing s Sparkz blind and cleaning out the office. When I say cleaning out, they cleaned him out. They took the computers, the debt, the Seventy inch Plasma T.V. out of the break room, the scripts, the messages, the camera system, the radio, coffee pots, all that kind of stuff. I mean, wiped him out. The printers and all. Now I know what you're thinking, man. What's the big deal? They took some scripts, some messages. That ain't no drug dealer shit. Well, those scripts and those messages are the golden words that the collectors or the hustlers use to make hundreds of thousands of dollars a month. Millions of dollars a year. It's like the dope dealer's recipe for the perfect Coke or the perfect drug. You don't want to risk the competition getting their greasy hands on those scripts. Every minute those collectors are on the phone using that script to get a payment, they're stripping the potency from it. It's the equivalent to the coach having his playbook stolen. All the years of hard work and trial and error, gone down the drain.

Your scripts and messages are your secret weapons. This shit is a blow to the gut. Taking a complete loss, while losing profits. It's just like the plug whose dealer runs off on him when he provided the trap house. Basically running away with all the drugs, all the scales, all the baggies, all the furniture in the trap house, the TVs, and leaving you with the rent to pay for the place. Also sticking you with the cost of restarting that operation. Leaving you to find a new group of hustlers, invest in more drugs, more scales, blah blah blah, all over again.

Fast forward to Tuesday morning. The day after Labor Day, Sparkz and his business partners were getting a million calls. Their cell phones were blowing up. The employees from Tina and Kevin's office were calling saying that they're at the office but no one is there. This was unusual because normally the managers or owners are at least thirty minutes to an hour early to get the day started. The employees were saying that the office was dark, and the doors were locked. It was now forty five minutes into the shift for when they were supposed to start. Everyone said they tried calling Tina and Kevin, but both of their phones were going straight to voicemail. Sparkz was furious. He knew what was cracking! He immediately drove to the office. Upon arrival he opened up the door only to find a ram sacked office along with a few computers, unplugged cords, papers scattered around and things of that nature. Sparkz didn't want the other employees to worry, so he basically told them to go ahead and go home. He would notify them when it's okay to return to work, and that he would also pay them for the day. Although they didn't work, everyone went home and enjoyed their day off. His next phone call was to the Goons and shit got real.

I got a call from Sparkz

"Hello"

"Yo..These motherfuckers just burned me." "Who? Wait…Whoa. What happened?" "Tina and Kevin's Bitch Ass. Yo, these muthafuckas took everything out of the office, man. They took my fuckin TVs, My computers and my debt! Yo, meet me at my spot at eight o'clock tonight, son." "All right, bro. I'm going to hit you back. I'm in the middle of training right now." In a rage Sparkz drove to Tina and Kevin's apartment. They had a little one bedroom in Conyers. He went over there banging on the door and ringing the doorbell, but no one answered. He continued to bang louder and louder. Still, no one answered. Their car wasn't there either. It was clear. They skipped town.

One thing that Tina and Kev didn't know that I did, is that Sparkz would kill him if he caught up to him. See, they never had a chance to hang out with them outside of work like I did. Once I got a chance to come into the fold, I soon realized that these were real street niggas who were just really good in collections and knew how to play the role. See, Sparkz had a lot of people from different races, and walks of life, coming in and out of the office.

Like this white dude named Frank that would always come in from time to time. I never knew who he was, but I knew he was important. On the days when Frank came in, Sparkz wore nice custom suits, dressing up like he's going to court or something. He would always fluff up the numbers (write additional payments) on the board and tell us to be on our best behavior. I believe Frank was a silent business partner or one of the clients. I could never figure out what a clean cut white guy was doing with a nigga like Sparkz. When he walked in, he never spoke to anyone. Looking really serious with his hands behind his back like he was handcuffed or something, he would stare at the numbers on the board, and then stare at the collectors. You would see him making small talk with Sparkz before they walked into his office, closing the door behind them. Sparkz always looked like he was on edge whenever Frank came in, but I say that to say he was a chameleon.

When with the homies.

He had a real grimy New York accent and used a whole bunch of slang. "You know what I mean Son?" "Fuck you! and Fuck this and that!" But he also had a real professional tone. Sounded like a teacher, like a preppy professional with a real liberal New York Wall Street type of accent as well. He was really good at playing both sides of the fence. Tina and Kev didn't realize that they were dealing with a wolf in sheep's clothing and that they could end up dead behind burning him. They probably figured that he would just sue them, or cut his losses. Yeah, he was going to sue them all right. I got another call from Sparkz after closing down the office. I was in the middle of wrapping up a meeting. "All right, y'all did a great job today. Remember we got to get on top of those declines. We had quite a few chargebacks.." My phone kept vibrating in my pocket. "Alright, I'll see you guys tomorrow. Hold it down." I took the call. "Hey, what's going on?" "Check this out, son. Don't worry about coming to the meeting tonight. I got another mission for you." "What's the move homie?" I asked, ready for whatever.

He said "I need you to lay on top of Tina and Kevin's apartment tonight! I'm going to come pick you up and have you drive one of the whips they neva seen before." I listened intensely. "You going to sit in the parking lot and watch their apartment for any type of movement?" "Say less" "I DONT GIVE A FUCK, if you see a FLY on top of their door! ANYTHING move inside that window, or if anybody comes to that house, you give me a call!" "Aight I got you." He finished his war cry. "Shit. Don't even worry about it either. I'ma tighten you up wit a little something for ya pockets too." "Don't even worry about it, G. This one is on the house, my nigga." "Aight, Good looking son. I'm going to hit you up before I come through." "Bet." Later on that evening, Sparkz came to pick me up in a black F-150. No rims, nothing fancy, just a standard pickup truck with tinted windows, like a working man's construction truck.

He told me this is what I would be using for the stake out. Also, to back in a parking space on the other side of the parking lot, where I could see the apartment. He said, "These muthufuckas probably skipped town already. But I just wanna be sure. Besides, they might slip up and come back tonight. They probably forgot somethin important, you feel me!?" "Yup!" I spent the night in the car talking on the phone, eating snacks and fast food, drinking beer, smoking and just chilling. They never did show up. Around six to seven o'clock in the morning. I ended up leaving as I did have

Debt, Guns, and Dope

to open the office for my crew. After all, I did still have to run my shop. Tina and Kevin were officially AWOL and were most wanted by the crew. They were officially on the hit list. Word began to surface around the office about what happened with Tina and Kev. Collections is a small world and word travels fast. The collectors began to whisper and make rumors about what took place. There was also another word being spread amongst the inner circle that if anybody could get in touch with Tina and Kev, or if anybody seen them, to let niggas know immediately as there will be grave consequences behind this shit. The cold part about it is this actually happens more than Sparkz would like it too. This wasn't the first rodeo.

He was now a victim of the finesse. He gave them debt that he may not be able to call because chances are the people have paid it, or Tina and Kevin are on their way to some remote location off the grid, to have a group of collectors closing on that debt. Doing numbers, making hundreds of thousands a month, all off of Sparkz money and the portfolio that he paid for. This can't be good. I was absolutely right. Shit was not good. I don't know if it's because I was still new to the crew and Sparks couldn't completely trust me, or maybe because he had bigger plans for me as an owner, but he never had me get my hands dirty. At least not yet. But I began hearing stories. Word got back that coincidentally Tina's mother's house was shot up. I'm not saying it was Sparkz and the crew, but it is coincidental. I also heard stories that one of Kevin's cousins was kidnapped and tortured. Nothing major though. They just sliced up his face with a razor. He ended up with a few broken ribs, a broken arm and they knocked out a few teeth. Things were getting really, really serious. All I did was kind of keep look out, and I was just told if I heard anything from Kevin and Tina to give them a call. Shit was heating up, Sparkz was going to track down his debt and his money by any means. He refused to let people play 'em.

The whispers amongst the crew is that he vowed not to let this shit go. He had a $10,000 bounty on their heads. At this point, it was about the principle. Also, his reputation was on the line as everybody was watching how we handled the situation. Although, this isn't the streets, the same rules had to be enforced. If you let somebody steal from you in the streets with no retaliation. That sends a signal to everybody else that you're an easy target. A free meal. Same shit applied here. If he didn't strike back, he became food. Sparkz was a big fish in the collection game. Owning and or having partnership in over twenty collection agencies, scattered across Georgia, Alabama and Tennessee. Also, having some people working remotely. Him and the crew is easily responsible for at least maybe 25 to 30% of all the debt that was being funneled through Atlanta. He's a big fish in the game with a lot of reach and pull. I continued to run my shop and handle business as normal. Keeping my platoon of collectors in shape, doing numbers and closing deals. Sparkz took in Tina and Kevin's collectors. He gave them jobs, at his different offices, based on the closest location to their home. On the other hand, Tina and Kevin officially became the most wanted collectors. Not in a good way though. They were on the hit list. I would not want to be in their shoes.

CH: 10 Some Extra Bread

MAD DAVENPORT

CHAPTER 10
SOME EXTRA BREAD

One foggy Sunday morning, I was posted at the gates, playing Madden on PS3. when I got a call from my boss/ business partner. I pressed start on the controller and answered, "Hello?" "Yo, what's good my nigga?" He said. "Shit, posted like a thumbtack playing Madden, what's the deal?" In his most gutted New York accent he said, "Please don't tell me you're playing with the bum ass chargers yo, hahaha."

Unpausing the game so he can hear the live action and frantically tapping on the keys on the joystick, I said, "Fuck you homie." I began to sing... "San Diegoooo Super chargerss.. we better than the Bills." The laughter faded away. "What you got goin on? I asked." Sparkz replied, "Nothing major..I really called to see, if you had wanted to make some extra bread." "Hell yeah homie, doing what?" "Man, breaking down cubicles and cleaning out the office, Tina and Kev was in. Im still tight, you know they fucking burnt me right!?" He asked angrily. Sparkz was so pissed off, he forgot that he deployed me to stake out their gates. "I got you my nig, yeah I remember. What time?" "Like, within the next hour or so, I can swing by and grab you. I'll pay you like $250, buy you lunch and all that shit." "For sure we can run it." "Aight, appreciate you my G! It shouldn't take long, we just gonna break down the cubicles, it's a few computers they left behind, a mini fridge...I think I got a coffee pot there. It ain't much. We'll just throw that shit in the back of the truck and we outta there."

"Let's go," I yelled at the TV. I confirmed rooting: "Good catch, Antonio. Okay, all right, I said low key, rushing him off the phone. I got you, I'm down, just hit me when you're outside." "Aight bet." "Gone." Tossing the phone on the floor, I finished the game and spanked the New England Patriots. I turned off the PlayStation and threw on an old t-shirt before Sparkz pulled up. While waiting, I opened up the fridge and grabbed a blue can that read Bud Ice. I cracked it open and began chugging. I picked up the remote and began flipping through the channels until I landed on my favorite channel. Bounce TV, the best network for people that didn't have cable.

About 45 minutes had passed by. I heard loud music getting closer and closer to my building second by second. Followed by the rumble of the bass. BOOM, BOOM, CLAP, BOOM, BOOM, BOOM, CLAP. Raekwon from the Wu-Tang Clan began rapping:

"Machine gun raps/ for all my niggas in the back/ stadium packed."

The music slowly faded away, and then my phone rang. "Hey, I'm out." Cutting him off mid-sentence. I said. "I know, you outside, nigga. I heard you pulling up from a mile away. Shit, everybody on Candler Rd know you outside!" Ha Ha Ha!! We laughed together. "Here I come." I hopped in the passenger seat of the black F-150 closing the door behind me. "What's up, homie?" I said, dapping up. "Tired as fuck, B! Was arguing wit wifey all last night. Plus, my nephew was supposed to really be doing this shit with you. His ass went to the Braves Game with his girl." He glanced in the rearview mirror. I said "Man, don't tell me wifey found out about your little breezy from PinUps (Strip Club)." "It is what it is. I just want to get this office cleaned out." He changed the subject and kept talking.

"I just want to get this office cleaned out, get those cubicles out of there, and I still need to get that Riverdale office going. They still Fuckin charging me rent for the office Tina and Kev was in!" The way he was venting and ranting, it was obvious he had allot on his mind and plate." I replied. "Everything gone work out Bro. The greatest quarterbacks in the game get Sacked sometimes! You feel me!?" "I know, this Shit, just happened at a Bad time. We're trying to get up 3 Million Dollars, so we can buy out and take over Golden Financial. They're based out of South Carolina. We get that office and we will have the streets on LOCK!" He smashed the gas and changed lanes. He carried on. "But yeah, this shouldn't take us no more than a few hours. Whatever desktops are still there, those can go to the new office that we're opening up in Buckhead in December. Man, that shit got enough space for like 30 collectors. Ughhh" Sparkz said, hella excited. "I'm telling you Monty, I'ma fill that bitch up with cheeks in seats and have everybody doing $15,000 to $20,000 a month. Word Up!" Seeing his vision I replied: "That's how you do it my nig!..Man, I'm trying to be like you when I grow up." He said, "Nah, you're going to be mad rich one day, Monty. You're smart and you're a hustler and you got business savvy. Real talk, and you're one of the best closers in the business. Trust me, kid, I know, I'm from Buffalo. Collection's Capital of the world, baby." "Man, I appreciate that Homie." I replied, feeling honored.

I respected and admired that about Sparkz. Even though he was rich, he was humble and he never looked down on me. He gave me a fist bump and said "No doubt, that's why I fuck with you. We here!" He cruised over the speed bumps that lined the street and pulled into the office plaza. He shifted in reverse and backed into a parking space, in front of a tinted glass door that read "Suite 207" in bold white lettering. We jumped out the car and walked in the office with a, well here goes nothing demeanor.

Mad Davenport

▇▇▇ COMMUNICATIONS RULES

Attendance: You are expected to be ready to work at 9:00am. If you are going to be out you need to contact ▇▇▇(404-▇▇▇) or ▇▇(678-▇▇▇) by voice or text message. No voice mails, don't send message through a co-worker.

Tardy: You are given a 15 minute grace period (do not abuse it). If you are going to be tardy contact ▇▇▇ or ▇▇ to inform what time you will be arriving.

Call Volume: You are required to make a minimum of 125 calls per day.

Declined Recoveries: You have 3 days to recover your declined payment. If you fail to recover declines they will be placed in managers desk & up for grabs.

File Toss: New business will be added in collectors desk after activation of previous accounts.

2nd Talk offs: If your account requires a second talk off, do not let consumer off the phone until you can get a 2nd t/o.

Disturbance: There will be no floor outbursts. If any disruption occurs that collector will face disciplinary actions up to possible termination.

Documentation: All accounts must be properly documented to receive credit for any payments.

Status Accounts: Make sure you properly status all accounts. This will allow you to protect your accounts & helps management assist you with good working accounts.

Green Money Contest: Any verified real time payment $100 or more. You will receive $5.00 for every $100 dollars you collect.

Debt, Guns, and Dope

I noticed Sparkz looking around the office with a look of disappointment and then sadness. I could tell it kinda hurt Sparkz that they violated his trust and stole from him like that. Especially when he tried to help them. We stood there quietly scanning the ram-sacked office. The look of disappointment and hurt transformed into a cold stare of anger and feeling betrayed. His face tensed up. He said, "Man, I can't believe these MUTHAFUCKAZ really PLAYED me! Stole my computers, ran off with my fucking debt. Millions of DOLLARS worth of fucking DEBT! Processing payments through their own merchant and shit." His fist was balled up. "Man, Ima fucking kill!, You know what?" He paused. "What's up?" I asked. He remained quiet, shaking his head. I followed his eyes, as he zoomed in on the blank space on the gray wall. He said "Yo, these greasy muthafuckaz took my paintings too!? Oh, hell naw.. Yo, Monty, do me a favor son. Can you run to the truck and grab my toolbox?" "Yeah, I got you, bro." I returned with the toolbox and dropped it on the carpet. "Yo, let's just get this shit done so I can get home and get some sleep. I cant believe these muthafuckas!" He said shaking his head. He opened up the toolbox, grabbed a flathead and handed me a rubber mallet. I gripped the back of the cubicle wall and we began to disassemble.

After a few hours of carrying partitions, file cabinets, desktop computers, and all kinds of knick-knacks to the truck, we finally had the truck loaded and packed to capacity. Swinging my arms in a circular motion and stretching, I said, "Ooh-whee. Man, I'ma sleep good tonight. I'm burnt out!" Leaning back in a computer chair, Sparkz replied, "Me too fam. I'ma take a nice, hot shower, eat dinner, and it's a wrap. Ugghh, ahhhh," He yawned and said "Hit that light switch." He picked up his toolbox. "Let's get the fuck out of here. I can have my nephew grab the rest of this shit tomorrow." We mobbed back to the truck and tracked out. I was so exhausted, I dozed off and slept the whole ride back. After a few taps on my left shoulder and a: "Yo Nigga we here" I was awake.

Chapter 10: Some Extra Bread

I unbuckled my seatbelt to the sound of crispy money being counted, and Sparkz mumbling, "60, 80, 81, 82, 83, 120, 40, 60. Here, this is like $190. I thought I had more cash on me. I'll shoot the rest to you on Monday at the office." I replied, "Man, I know your rich ass is good for it. I aint trippin. Quiet is kept, I really could use a new computer. My shit running hella slow. Can I get one of those desktops back there? and we call it even" He didn't blink. "Yeah, we can do that. Grab one from back there." I grabbed a Dell monitor, hard drive, mouse, keyboard, and all the necessary cords.

Lugging the Dell up upstairs, Sparkz Shouted, "Yo!" He wagged his finger in a come here type motion. "Yo, put that shit back." He said, referring to the computer I had in hand. "I wanna see you right out here. Grab that Mac from back there. The screen is cracked, but you get the screen fixed and you rocking and rolling. Plus, Apple is the wave of the future my nigga. Like you tell people at the office. Get ya Barz up! (impersonating my voice)" I laughed and picked up the gold-plated monitor, a lighter hard drive with a sleek white mouse. "Ayy, good-looking homie!" I said, walking up the stairs. He tapped the horn twice going in reverse before he took off. He said, "Check you out on Monday, Hold it down!" Throwing the peace sign up out the window as he rolled off into the sunset.

CHAPTER 11: The Alphabet Boys

Mad Davenport

CHAPTER 11
THE ALPHABET BOYS

In the Dope Game, the dealer is always ducking and dodging the FBI, DEA, ATF, and the IRS. Oh yeah, and the PDs for the local dealers. Whether you're a featherweight hustler with an 8 ball of coke or the head of a multi-million dollar drug smuggling ring, one of your worst nightmares is having the Alphabet Boys raid your home and/or businesses. Shit, you don't even want to be on their radar.

Well in collections, we have our set of Alphabet Boys that we're ducking and dodging too. The FTC (Federal Trade Commission) which is our version of the FBI, and the CFPB (Consumer Financial Protection Bureau) which is an independent group of attorneys. Both of these agencies make it their business to go after rogue collection agencies or any telemarketing company that use unfair, abusive, deceptive, or antitrust practices to get money out of a consumer.

The FTC enforces a variety of antitrust and consumer protection laws, affecting damn near every area of commerce.

The FTC has a list of banned collection agencies. If you want to, go to www.ftc.gov or Google FTC banned collection agencies, and you'll be sure to find a list of people and companies banned by federal court orders from participating in the business of debt collections.

This is easily circumvented though. The ambitious and savvy collection agency owner will simply open up a trap (office) under a new name. With a trusted friend, family member or whoever to be listed as the owner. They can easily get a new 1-800 number, New P.O. Box, with a new group of collectors (and few previous employees). Bada-Boom, with one phone call to the plug or the debt broker, they're right back in business.

Chapter 11: The Alphabet Boys

Depending on what type of collection agency owner you're dealing with, determines how they bounce back after an FTC raid. You have collection agency owners who were once a collector themselves, meaning they started off in a cubicle. They're capable of getting on the phones and generating $10,000 to $15,000 plus a month themselves.

Then you have collection agency owners who never hammered the phones, but had the money to invest, stumbled into collections by a friend, or however they may have got into the business. They are normally the ones who can get back in business on the backs of other collectors, as long as they got debt or work.

Sparkz, he was part of the elite group that started off in the cubicle as a collector. He was capable of getting in a cubicle and doing $20,000 a month easily. At any given time in the office, he would take a second Talk -Off (take over call to help the collector close the deal). Just to show he still got it. That's what separated him from other collection agency owners. I also believe that's why he had empathy towards us, because he was in the cubicle hammering the phones day in and day out too, at one point. He knows how it feels and what it takes to get the job done. Similar to football coaches who actually played football.

Typically, when collection agency owners start off in the cubicle, they're more on the side of the collector and tend to have better bonus structures with higher payouts. Along with sweet incentives for you to make a few extra bucks. They understand what fuels a collector. Normally if an agency owner has never hammered the phones, they tend to treat you like slaves in a sweatshop. "Hammer the phones, take these calls, make these calls, smile and dial, collect, collect, collect!" But rarely do they reciprocate with nice bonuses.

Now I know what you're thinking, the FTC ain't the FBI, true, but you don't want them doing forensics on your computers, looking into your payroll records, your books, seizing your hard drives. Aside from shutting down your business and your office, these motherfuckers yield the power to have a federal judge put a restraining order on your office, only permitting you access to go there one day out of the week for a few hours to gather your belongings. That's after they ransack your office, leaving papers and debris all over the place.

Oh, did I forget to mention they can freeze your business assets and individual assets. Aside from that, when the FTC raids your trap, it has a trickle down effect. The owner loses his or her business. Employees can't get paid. They lose their job. The debtor, they aren't allowed to make payments. Also, they don't get a chance to clear their credit and they lose all the monies that they've paid thus far to start clearing their debt. In so many words... When the FTC raids your office, it's similar to the FBI raiding the home of the kingpin, except with less guns and no SWAT team.

Agency owners are paranoid about them crashing the party. They don't want the FTC and their investigators coming in. When they storm your spot, they come in with plain clothes, badges, local police and all. They normally come in unexpectedly in the afternoon. They come in and yell, "Everybody step away from the computer." And everyone gets handcuffs as they search the office for who runs the show.

Everyone is processed, has their photos taken, and they will eventually be told to leave immediately as long as they don't have any warrants. At that juncture, a temporary restraining order is issued, preventing company employees from stepping on the premises, seeing any company files or financial records. Crazy right?

While all this is taking place, as the agency owner, you better pray to God that you don't have any other criminal activity going on, because at that point they will discover it. I say all that to say shit just hit the fan. Sparkz worst nightmare just became a reality.

Our office was raided! Unbeknownst to us, we were being investigated for countless complaints to the FTC. They had received countless calls from debtors, stating that they were threatened with warrants, and possible jail time if they failed to pay their bill. Things finally came collapsing. The smoking gun was a rookie closer, violating one of the most important rules in the collection handbook. You don't say anything, and I mean anything, violating the FDCPA on a voicemail. Not saying it's okay to say it on a live call, but at least on a live call it's he say, she say. Plus, you could dance in a gray area, meaning say something illegal, but not saying it at the same time. An innuendo, Painting the picture of the consequences or what could happen.

Once it is on a voicemail, it's recorded, documented, and there's nothing you can say to change it. Anyways, this new booty collector left something on a voicemail, along the lines of "Due to non-payment. We may have to process a notice for you to appear in court. It's mandatory that you set up a payment plan with our attorneys. Call us immediately to stop a possible warrant." This guy was just making a gumbo out of legal terms and statements he heard around the office from the real Top Gun Closers. What this jackass didn't know is, this message would be sent to the FTC along with our phone number and P.O. Box. That message was the straw that broke the camel's back. We were officially on the FTC's radar, and soon to be plastered on their website as a banned collection agency.

Chapter 11: The Alphabet Boys

On a humid Wednesday morning around 11ish, I was drinking a cup of coffee and flirting with the girl who sat in the cubicle next to me. "Girl, Stop playing and let me give you some of this California love." She giggled like a schoolgirl, "Boy yo ass is throwed off."

In the midst of my game, we heard the dreadful words that no agent wants to hear. "Everybody back away from the computers and don't touch anything! This office is officially under seizure by the United States Federal Trade Commission! We have an order signed by a federal judge. As long as everybody complies and does what we ask, we will get you out of here as soon as possible." Yelled a white man in a strong law enforcement tone of voice.

He was accompanied by other agents and a team of investigators along with the Atlanta Police Department. They had badges hanging from around their necks, wearing blue jeans and wearing breaker jackets.

All the office chatter sizzled down to silence and all smiles turned to looks of fear and uncertainty as we were rounded up one by one, zip tied with our hands behind our back and escorted to the front by the Alphabet Boys for processing.

While this is taking place, investigators aggressively yanked computer cords from wall sockets. They then proceeded to pull down every script and/or notes hung up in the cubicle after grabbing the hard drives and monitors to be boxed up and processed.

It was now my turn to face the music. They brought me to the conference room and removed the zip ties from my wrist. They had me sit down in the computer chair across from the head honcho (Lead Investigator). "What's your name?" "Lamont Davenport." He jotted in the notepad without looking up at me. He asked, "How long have you been employed here?" "About Six months." He continued to write. "What's your position?" "Collection representative." He looked up at me. "You got some Identification on you?" I swiveled in the chair and dug into my pocket to grab the wallet that held my I.D. I handed it to him. Smacking his lips and scoffing: "California, huh?"

He signaled to the agent that guarded the door. With eye contact and a head nod, the agent unfolded his arms and came to grab my I.D. out of the agent's hands. He vanished out of the room and stayed gone for a few minutes. They were letting me cook. After a few follow-up questions, they returned my I.D. and released me. "You're free to go."

Shaking up, heart beating fast and sweaty, I moseyed out of the office to the sight of Sparkz, handcuffed in the back of the blue Atlanta police car. It was clear he was headed to jail. As I walked to the bus stop, we made eye contact. Although we couldn't talk, his eyes were speaking volumes. They were saying, "I really fucked up this time and I'm sorry it went down like this." He looked nervous.

Chapter 11: The Alphabet Boys

I stood in front of the weather-worn bus stop, spaced out and feeling lost. The whole bus ride home, I replayed the raid in my head along with different schemes to come up with some cheese since I was out of a job and rent was still due.

Word got back that they charged the collector who left the message with impersonating law enforcement and threatening consumers. He will be summoned to appear in the Supreme Court in the state of New York. A few other Closers were arrested too.

Most of my coworkers were released within the hour. We were all shitting bricks to the thought of the FTC listening to the recordings that we had left. Paranoid, reflecting on all the things that we had said to make people pay. Thankfully, Sparkz didn't have the calls recorded. He was using that as a scare tactic to make sure that we were doing things by the book.

After the smoke cleared, rumors began to surface that Sparkz was facing serious time for wire fraud and attempted murder back in New York. Collections is a small world and word travels fast.

When I heard the news, I took it with a grain of salt because the truth of the matter is they didn't know the Boss outside of work. As collectors they weren't privy to the behind the scenes logistics. It was just pure speculation and gossip.

About five days and some change after the FTC raided the trap, I got a call from Sparkz. "You have a collect call from an inmate in a Fulton County Correctional Facility. To accept these charges, press 1 now." I immediately smashed 1. "Yo, what's up my nigga!?" "Monty, what's good, yo?" "Holding on like a toupee in the wind! Trying to make somethin shake. How you holding up in there bro?" Sparkz replied "Shit..I'm good fam, better than ever! My paper is straight. I got one of the best attorneys in the United States working my case. I'm Gucci!" "That's right!" I said. See, in jail you never want the ear hustlers to overhear you sounding stressed out, possibly scared or worried. He continued "But yo..I tapped your line to tell you, I think you need to go home and see your family. I know they miss you kid. And I know yo ass miss that good ass Cali bud and the beaches. Enjoy your life. Go take a vacation son."

His tone alerted me that he was hinting at something. Like if he was saying the shit in front of me, he would be winking an eye. The recording interrupted him "This call is being monitored and or recorded." In a combative tone, Sparkz shouted: "WHAT MUTHAFUCKA! Yea' alright we'll see about that!" He was barking at an inmate in the background, who was pressing him about something. "But yo…Much love Monty, hold it down." "Much love homie. I got you. keep ya head up in there." "You already know! We'll be in touch though. I'll call you when I get up top. I'm just waiting to be extradited back to New York right now. Don't forget what I said though son. Go home!" Hanging up the phone, I read in between the lines. Sparkz was basically telling me to get out of dodge. Shit just got real!

TO BE CONTINUED

Debt, Guns & Dope
                PT. 2
            The RE-UP

WRITTEN BY: MAD DAVENPORT